The

SCIENCE of KISSING

The

SCIENCE

of

KISSING

What Our Lips Are Telling Us

Sheril Kirshenbaum

GRAND CENTRAL
NEW YORK   PUBLISHING   BOSTON

Grand Central Publishing
Hachette Book Group
237 Park Avenue
New York, NY 10017

www.HachetteBookGroup.com

Book design by Fearn Cutler de Vicq
Printed in the United States of America

First Edition: January 2011
10 9 8 7 6 5 4 3 2 1

Grand Central Publishing is a division of Hachette Book Group, Inc.
The Grand Central Publishing name and logo is a trademark of
Hachette Book Group, Inc.

Library of Congress Cataloging-in-Publication Data

Kirshenbaum, Sheril.
The science of kissing : what our lips are telling us / Sheril
Kirshenbaum.—1st ed.
p. cm.
Includes bibliographical references and index.
ISBN 978-0-446-55990-4
1. Kissing.   I. Title.
GT2640.K567 2011
394—dc22   2010009535

For David, who inspires me every day

Contents

PART THREE

Great Expectations

"Is this a kissing book?"

—*The Princess Bride*, 1987

Preface

A kiss is one of the most significant exchanges two people can have, serving as an unspoken language to convey our deepest feelings when words simply will not do. From a symbol of love and desire to a perfunctory greeting between family and friends, this act can have innumerable meanings and resonances. For many of us, it is part of our earliest introduction to planet earth, and is often involved in our final exit as well. Some kisses are sealed forever in our minds and hearts, while others are forgotten as quickly as they occur. Across continents and time, kissing is one of the most important activities in our lives, yet its real nature has been too often overlooked by scientists and laypeople alike.

When I first told friends and colleagues I was working on this book, many of them wondered aloud what would inspire a project on osculation—the scientific term for kissing. But I turned the question around: Why not? After all, decades ago, anthropologists estimated that kissing was practiced by over 90 percent of cultures around the world. The figure has probably grown thanks to globalization, the Internet, and the ease with which we now course across hemispheres. Even in societies in which couples do not traditionally kiss, they frequently engage in similar behaviors, such as licking or nibbling at one another's faces and bodies. This makes kissing a practice with obvious evolutionary significance, whose study could provide insight into our collective past and current physiology. And given that kissing also leaves such an indelible mark on the human experience, why not further explore this behavior from as many angles as possible?

My journey toward writing this book began in 2008. The week before Valentine's Day, I composed a short piece, entitled "The Science of Kissing," at The Intersection, the *Discover* magazine blog I share with science journalist Chris Mooney. To our surprise, readership spiked as the page was linked widely around the Internet. We received thousands of visitors over the next several days, and emails poured in with questions. They never stopped.

By Valentine's Day 2009, I had co-organized a panel discussion on "The Science of Kissing" for the normally staid annual meeting of the American Association for the Advancement of Science. The press went wild scheduling briefings, and our kissing symposium was covered by major news outlets ranging from National Geographic to CNN, making headlines in countries all around the world.

Everyone seemed curious to hear what a bunch of scientists had to say about something so obviously relevant to each of our lives.

As the kissing queries continued, I dug into some books to see what was out there. The answer was, not much. The standard how-to manuals contained few answers to my growing list of questions. I wanted some solid explanations about why we kiss, what happens to our bodies when we do, and what this information might teach us about kissing in relationships. So I began interviewing experts, reading the scientific literature, and collecting theories. Some focused on chemical interactions during a kiss that may help us determine whether we have made a good match. Others tried to uncover kissing's origins by looking to our ancient ancestors' sexual exploits and preferences. It turned out there was a lot of interesting research related to kissing, but it was all in fragments.

As my investigation progressed, though, the science from different fields began to converge. Neuroscientists trying to understand how our brains function were interested to hear what endocrinologists reported on hormonal changes related to kissing. In turn, those same endocrinologists asked what I was hearing from anthropologists about similar behavior in other primates, like chimpanzees and bonobos. The anthropologists were curious to know what physiologists were finding about the body's physical response to a kiss. And so on.

Accessing the scientific literature on this subject, however, posed challenges of its own. I frequently found myself in awkward conversations with petite, elderly librarians that went something like this:

"Can you please help me find the article called 'Fetishes and Their Associated Behaviors'?"

"I'm sorry, did you say 'Fetishes'?"

"Yes, please."

"Here's the reference, dear. I won't ask what this is for, but be careful."

My research also garnered endless curious and at times incriminating glances from strangers as I reviewed related art and historical accounts on my laptop. On top of that, I discovered that mountains of misinformation have been circulating for years on kissing, with no scientific basis. And then there were the pursuits that led me to wander into very unfamiliar territory, such as when I interviewed a sex-robot engineer and viewed my brain in the laboratory. Needless to say, I could not have possibly imagined what I was getting into when I set out to write this book.

Fortunately, as I began composing the actual manuscript, a serendipitous coincidence brought me to San Francisco just in time to catch Mary Roach, author of *Bonk: The Curious Coupling of Science and Sex*, on her book tour. I was relieved to hear about Roach's struggles through similarly embarrassing situations, and listened intently as she discussed the challenges of writing on related topics. I took her words to heart, feeling inspired to press on. I had already been influenced by the works of sex research pioneers like Alfred Kinsey, William Masters, Virginia Johnson, and many others. If these brave individuals could go all the way when it came to exploring sexuality, surely I could at least aim for first base.

If a book on kissing raises some eyebrows, I can live with that. So with an open mind, several scientists in tow as allies, and a few inspired ideas, I embarked on the journey to understand the kiss—and learned more than I could have possibly imagined.

This book tells the true story of humanity's most intimate exchange.

XX

Sheril Kirshenbaum, January 2011

Any man who can drive safely while kissing a pretty girl
is simply not giving the kiss the attention it deserves.

—Albert Einstein

The
SCIENCE
of
KISSING

Introduction

Scientists are not exactly sure why we kiss. This may be in part because they have not even definitively decided what a kiss is. Unlike most other areas of scientific investigation, there's no accepted "taxonomy," or classification system, for different kinds of kisses and closely related behaviors. What's more, you don't find the experts crunching the numbers and figures on kissing across world cultures, as researchers would surely do if they wanted to get a handle on the available data. Why so little analysis of osculation? Perhaps kissing seems so commonplace that few of us have paused to reflect on its deeper significance. Or it's possible the subject has been intentionally avoided under the microscope given the challenges of interpreting what a kiss really means.

Yet the behavior we recognize as kissing simply cries out for better scientific explanation. Just think: From a completely clinical perspective, microbiologists will tell you that it is a means for two people to swap mucus, bacteria, and who knows what else. Picturing all those tiny organisms swishing through our saliva isn't just unromantic, it inspires a question: Why would this mode of transferring germs evolve? And why is it so enjoyable when the chemistry is right?

When it comes to kissing, there are also immediate and personal reasons for wanting to explore the science. It can help us understand how much kissing really matters in relationships, and whether we can enhance them by improving our technique. Are we born knowing how to kiss, or does practice make perfect? Do men and women experience kissing the same way? Why can a bad kiss stop a promising relationship cold, whereas the right one can begin something special with the person we least expect?

Because a kiss brings two individuals together in an exchange of sensory information by way of taste, smell, touch, and possibly even silent chemical messengers called pheromones (odorless airborne signals), it has the potential to provide all kinds of insight into another person. So even when our conscious minds may not recognize it, the act can reveal clues about a partner's level of commitment and possibly his or her genetic suitability for producing children.

The human body's response to kissing is just one of many intriguing aspects of the science involved. From an evolutionary perspective, scientists can't fully make up their minds whether humans kiss out of instinct, or if instead it's a learned behavior for expressing affection. The dispute traces back to none other than the father of evolutionary biology, Charles Darwin. In his 1872 book *The Expression of the Emotions in Man and Animals*, Darwin noted with interest that kissing "is replaced in various parts of the world, by the rubbing of noses." Here I introduce a distinction that will be important in later chapters. This is the difference between kissing with the lips and various "kissing-like behaviors" that may appear related and could serve similar purposes, or even represent a precursor to modern romantic kissing.

The definition of a kiss is relatively simple: It is either the mouth-to-mouth orientation of two individuals or the pressing of one's lips on some other part of another's body (or on an object). But "kissing-like behaviors" is a much broader category, and should include a large array of exchanges between people (or animals) that focus on the use of the lips and face, and perhaps some other body parts. For example, Darwin described the practice—very common in many cultures—of sniffing another human being in close contact, in search of recognition or to establish a rapport. Despite such cultural diversity, however, he suggested that the many different types of kisses and related behaviors found around the globe all reflected an innate desire to receive "pleasure from close contact with a beloved person."

In its broadest sense, then, Darwin surmised that the drive to "kiss" was innate and perhaps hereditary—or as we would now say, encoded in our genes.

Today some anthropologists disagree, maintaining that

kissing is a purely cultural phenomenon—a learned behavior that we pick up merely by watching others do it. The majority of experts, though, seem to share Darwin's original view, especially when using his broad definition, which groups together kissing with practices that included "the rubbing or patting of the arms, breasts, or stomachs," as well as "one man striking his own face with the hands or feet of another." From this vantage point, kissing-like behaviors appear nearly universal among human beings. And as we'll see, they have so many analogs in other species that they are likely part of our common evolutionary inheritance.

To fully explore the scientific kiss, this book takes its inspiration from an approach originally popularized by the late Dutch ethologist Nikolaas Tinbergen. Tinbergen emphasized that in order to understand a particular behavior, we should ask a specific set of questions about it. The answers to these questions are not mutually exclusive but instead serve to inform one another.

Part 1 of this book will explore what Tinbergen called the "ultimate" explanations for kissing—those that center on the behavior's evolutionary history and purpose. Here I will describe the leading theories that might account for how and why early humans started locking lips. Were we the first species on the planet to do so, or have we inherited the behavior from a shared ancestor with other mammals? By comparing human kissing with similar behaviors in other animals, we'll gain insight into how and why kissing emerged.

Next I will move on to examine kissing throughout human history and across modern cultures. At the end of this survey, you will see that while kissing-like behaviors take a vast number of forms, and while kissing norms in the world today vary greatly across societies, the basic desire to embrace another individual using the face, mouth, and sometimes other related parts of the body does appear to be universal, just as Darwin concluded. I'll come to terms with the famous "nature/nurture" debate by showing that the way we kiss is conditioned both by our biology and culture—the result being a fascinating variety of unique kissing styles, customs, and techniques.

But in a sense, that's just the prelude to the heart of the book. Part 2 explores how kissing is actually experienced in our bodies, an analysis that will allow us to consider what Tinbergen called the "proximate" explanations for this behavior. That means looking at kissing in its immediate context among individuals, and seeking to understand the neurological, biological, or psychological reasons underlying the motivation to kiss. Here I will also explore how the act of kissing directly affects an individual and the role it plays in the relationships he or she chooses, and chooses *not*, to have. We'll also learn about some major differences in how men and women perceive kissing, and the hidden information that kisses can convey.

Part 3 builds upon the lessons learned by moving into an actual laboratory setting to try to make some new discoveries about the science of kissing. In this, I'll enlist the help of a group of brave neuroscientists from New York University, who set up a novel MEG (magnetoencephalography) experiment using a cutting-edge scientific machine whose interior nevertheless looks remarkably like a toilet. From there, we'll glimpse at what the future of kissing itself may look like in our increasingly interconnected, digitized, and even robotic world. Finally, I'll synthesize themes throughout the book to provide some practical advice based on the best kissing research to date.

The ideas and theories on kissing that you'll read in these pages may be numerous, but unlike on popular reality television shows, we don't necessarily need to eliminate all the alternatives in order to isolate a winning contender. Rather, we'll explore kissing through many lenses at once, and you'll soon see that it's possible to tie seemingly unrelated fields of science together in unexpected and intriguing ways. By the end of the journey, you'll know vastly more about what's behind a kiss—but I promise, this knowledge won't take any of the magic away.

PART ONE

The Hunt

for

Kissing's Origins

I wonder what fool it was that first invented kissing.

—Jonathan Swift

CHAPTER I

First Contact

W hen it comes to humanity's first kiss, or its predecessor in another species, we have no way of knowing exactly how and why, once upon a time, it happened. After all, there are kisses of joy, of passion and lust, of love and endearment, of commitment and comfort, of social grace and necessity, of sorrow and supplication. It would be silly to assume all these different types of kisses developed from a single behavior or cause; in all likelihood, we kiss as we do today for *multiple* reasons, not just one. In fact, scientists suspect that kissing arose and disappeared around the globe at different times and different places throughout history.

So while there are certainly some convincing theories out there about how kissing may have emerged, nobody claims that they represent absolute truth. At best, they possess a degree of plausibility that makes them persuasive. In this chapter, we'll survey four such theories, each of which has a basis in the scientific literature.

Scientists have proposed two separate relationships between kissing and our feeding experiences in infancy and early childhood. They have also suggested that kissing may have emerged from the practice of smelling another individual of the species as a means of recognition. I will examine each of these theories, but will begin with perhaps the most intriguing one of all: the idea that the behavior arose due to a complex connection between color vision, sexual desire, and the evolution of human lips.

A WOMAN'S LIPS make an indelible impression. They draw attention to her face, advertising her assets in deeply hued and rosy colors. The effect is further enhanced because human lips are "everted," meaning that they purse outward. This trait sets us apart from other members of the animal kingdom. Unlike other primates, the soft, fleshy surface of our lips remains exposed, making their shape and composition intensely alluring.

But what makes them so attractive that we want to kiss the lips of another person?

A popular theory takes us back millions of years, when our ancestors had to locate food among leaves and brush. Calories were hard to come by, and wandering far into the jungle could be dangerous. In this context, some of our ancestors evolved a superior ability to detect reddish colors, giving them the advantage of locating the ripest fruits, which in turn helped them survive long enough to pass on their color-detecting genes to their offspring. Over many generations, the signal "red equals reward" became hard-wired into our ancestors' brains. Indeed, the color continues to grab our attention today—something marketing professionals know and exploit regularly.

Contemporary psychologists report that looking at red quickens the heart rate and pulse, making us feel excited or even "out of breath." In fact, red seems so important to humans that time and again, across early cultures, it is one of the first colors to be named. In their 1969 book *Basic Color Terms: Their Universality and Evolution*, anthropologist Brent Berlin and linguist Paul Kay studied twenty languages and determined that after cultures develop words for black and white (probably because these help to determine day from night), red is frequently the third.

But how does this relate to kissing? Neuroscientist Vilayanur S. Ramachandran of the University of California, San Diego, suggests that once our ancestors were primed to seek red for a food reward, they were probably going to check out the source of this color wherever it occurred—including on parts of the female anatomy. Eventually, red likely served as a flashy signal to help facilitate another essential and enjoyable behavior besides eating: *sex*.

Comparative evolutionary research has demonstrated that in primates, skin and hair coloring evolved *after* color vision. In other words, once our ancestors developed the ability to detect this color, it became emphasized on their bodies and particularly in the labial region, serving to indicate a female's peak period of fertility, called estrus. Those with the most conspicuous sexual swellings were probably also most successful at attracting males and passed their flamboyantly endowed posteriors on to their daughters. Today, there's no mistaking the females of many species when they are ready to mate. As Duke University primate scientist Vanessa Woods puts it, "Female bonobos look like they are carrying their own bright red bean bag attached to their bottoms to sit down on when they get tired."

But how did an attraction to the color red move from our nether regions to our facial lips? The most likely scenario is that when our ancestors stood upright, their bodies underwent many associated changes in response, including a shift in the location of prominent sexual signals. Over time, the delectable rosy color, already so attractive to males, shifted from our bottoms to our faces through a process called evolutionary co-option. And the male gaze followed.

That's why human females do not have to advertise our reproductive cycle on our rear ends. We exhibit what's called "hidden estrus" instead. But following this theory, our lips are quite literally a "genital echo," as the British zoologist Desmond Morris put it, resembling the female labia in their texture, thickness, and color. Indeed, when men and women become sexually excited, both our lips and our genitals swell and redden as they are engorged with blood, becoming increasingly sensitive to touch.

To test the "genital echo" hypothesis, Morris showed male volunteers photographs of women wearing various lipstick colors and asked them to rate the attractiveness of each. The men consistently chose those featuring the brightest (most aroused-looking) red lips as most appealing. To quote Morris, "These lipstick manufacturers did not create an enhanced mouth; they created a pair of super labia."

And if a plump, rosy smile gets noticed, it probably means men themselves are rewarded for paying attention—in an evolutionary sense. A woman's naturally large, reddish lips may provide clues about her fertility. They swell when she reaches puberty, and thin with age. Multiple studies have linked full lips to higher levels of the hormone estrogen in adult women, meaning that they serve as a reliable indicator of her reproductive capacity.

No wonder that across cultures, men report that fuller lips on women are an asset, and in turn women have recognized for millennia that there's power in highlighting them. The first record of lipstick dates back five thousand years to the Sumerian region, and ancient Egyptians,

Greeks, and Romans used dyes and strong wines to tint their lips.

Today's men continue to respond to the stimulus of a sexy mouth, and many women are eager—even desperate—to achieve Angelina Jolie–like proportions. Not only do 75 to 85 percent of American women wear lipstick, but we are taking the obsession to new extremes. We purchase plumpers to achieve the "beestung effect," and purposely irritate our outer lip membranes with everything from cinnamon to alpha hydroxy acids and retinol. We coat our mouths with formulas from sheep glands and regularly inject fillers and fat. Some women even insert Gore-Tex strips through painful lip implant procedures, which are increasing in popularity (even though a partner can sometimes feel them during a kiss). In the end, women are paying billions of dollars for a result that may be driven by the same impulses that first attracted our primate ancestors to ripe fruit.

Granted, the science suggests that all those fancy creams and glosses actually work . . . up to a point, anyway. According to psychologist Michael Cunningham of the University of Louisville, men really do prefer larger lips. However, they also report that fake-looking lips are a turnoff, suggesting that the size of a woman's mouth in relation to her other facial features is most important. Therefore, when those natural proportions are upset through cosmetic surgery, the result may not be as attractive as the original package.

So it's true: Our lips probably did evolve to look the way they do because they elicit a magnetic sexual attraction. But in the quest to understand the origins of kissing, there's a lot more ground (and face) to cover.

FOR THE NEXT THEORY, we need to consider the development of a human baby. During the first trimester in the womb, it will develop recognizable lips, and even before birth, fetuses have been observed to suck their thumbs. Upon delivery, newborns immediately form their mouths as if to nurse, which in a mechanical sense is the movement associated with kissing.

Noting as much, Desmond Morris had another idea about our lips. Aside from a "genital echo," he was interested in the way their shape makes them very well suited to suckle milk from the distinct human breast.

When our ancestors began to stand upright, red lips weren't the only sexual signal to migrate across our bodies. Female breasts also became more pronounced, mirroring the look of buttocks. While all mammals provide milk to their young through nursing, the rounded human breast has a unique contour. Unlike in species covered with hair, a woman's naked breasts stand out, drawing attention to her nipples.

During pregnancy, the breasts become swollen and tender. When the baby is born, a mother holds it close during feedings and the newborn responds by engulfing the nipple in his or her mouth. This encourages sucking behavior as the infant ingests vital nutrients needed to grow. Nursing is enormously pleasurable for the child, and new mothers quickly recognize that it's a great way to soothe and calm a fussy baby.

Given the critical importance of keeping infants well nourished, it's not surprising that evolution would shape the human nipple and lips so that they fit comfortably together. Furthermore, breast-feeding promotes a deep bond between a caregiving mother and her completely dependent baby through a flood of chemical messengers in their brains called neurotransmitters (which I'll discuss further in chapter 5). Here is the first encounter with safety and love, and Morris hypothesized that throughout our lives we associate lip pressure with these feelings. Later in life, we will seek similar experiences in other relationships, and kissing will come to promote a special connection between family members as well as between lovers. It allows us to convey warmth and affection through an expression we began to experience in infancy.

There has been a great deal of literature about the importance of the relationship between mother and child, and how this may dictate other encounters throughout our lives. Some readers will note that with this theory of kissing's origins, we are approaching terrain popularized by Sigmund Freud. He, too, proposed that the drive to kiss begins during infancy. The child, once deprived of its mother's breast, seeks similar pleasurable sensations throughout its lifetime through thumb-sucking and other behaviors. As Freud put it, "The inferiority of this second region [the thumb] is among the reasons why at a later date he seeks the corresponding part—the lips—of another person ('It's a pity that I can't kiss myself,' he seems to be saying)." According to Freud, we spend our lives trying to return to our mother's breast.

The big difference between the views of Freud and Morris is that while Freud viewed kissing as a symptom of breast deprivation, Morris described it as a way of rekindling positive experiences from infancy. Although we do not have clear memories of our earliest years, puckering up to nurse in a mother's comforting embrace probably does have a lasting impact on us, as lip contact itself becomes entwined with feelings of love and trust.

OF COURSE, THERE'S MORE to feeding a growing child than breast milk or formula, and kissing theories also abound that originate in the next stage of development following infancy.

For thousands of years, "premastication"—the pre-chewing of a meal for another individual—served as a central means of delivering food to young, largely helpless toddlers. A premasticating mother places her mouth over her child's and parts both lips. Then, using her tongue, she presses soft food between them.

While this practice may sound unappetizing to some, it's important to remember that for most of our existence, mothers had far fewer options than they do now. Daniel and Dorothy Gerber didn't start hand-straining solids in their kitchen until 1927, and grocery stores stocking prepared jars of mashed peas haven't speckled our landscapes until rather recently. Premastication was the most practical way to wean children off breast milk before they had a full set of teeth.

Written records of prechewing food date back to ancient Egypt. But humans have probably been feeding each other this way since prehistoric times and, indeed, the behavior likely comes to us from our nonhuman ancestors, like great apes. It occurs in other parts of the animal kingdom as well, as I'll discuss in the next chapter.

In fact, premastication persists in human cultures even today. A recent survey reported that people in 39 out of 119 modern cultures studied premasticate a wide array of substances, citing food exchange, healing rituals, disease prevention, and more. However, it is important to note that kissing is not necessarily present in all cultures where the prechewing of food occurs. For example, premastication was long practiced among the Ituri Pygmies of the Congo, yet mouth-to-mouth kissing was apparently unknown among these peoples until Europeans arrived.

Nevertheless, just as with nursing, premastication may lay the foundation for kissing behaviors later in life. We've already seen how oral stimulation in infancy helps foster loving feelings and strong attachments. The premastication theory is, in essence, just an extension of this logic. Past the nursing stage, the child continues to develop and receive care from a loving mother, and now the oral stimulation occurs in a mouth-to-mouth fashion. The intense bond comes to center on contact at the lips—and quite possibly a pattern of behavior and emotional response is established that will help promote kissing much later in the child's life.

In this way, it is possible that through repeated puckering between mothers and children, the passionate romantic kiss between lovers could have emerged.

THE NURSING AND PREMASTICATION hypotheses suggest that our ancient guide for intimacy may lie in something far less romantic—suckling a mother's breast, sharing pre-chewed food along with our saliva, or some combination of both. However, there is also evidence that kissing may originate with a very different facial feature: our noses. The friendly and familial variant of the kiss could have started with a *sniff*.

Humans have powerful scent glands under our skin, giving each of us a distinct smell. Scientists have observed that even in infancy, human beings use their noses to keep track of important relationships. Breast-fed newborns, for example, seem able to recognize their mother's natural odor, while bottle-fed babies do not develop the ability.

In a similar way, many anthropologists believe that the first "kisses" may have been delivered via our noses rather than our lips, as we closely inhaled the scent of our loved ones' cheeks. Many early cultures became accustomed to what's called the "oceanic kiss," so named to describe a traditional greeting in Polynesia. Such a "kiss" involves going back and forth across the nose to smell another person for the purpose of identification, and probably served as a reliable means to recognize and reconnect with relatives and friends, and perhaps even provide clues about a person's health.

Over time, a brush of the lips may have come to accompany this practice—eventually leading to the evolution of kissing as a greeting. This could have started the tradition of the social kiss, in which we welcome friends and community members, sending the message that we're glad to see them or have missed their company.

It's important to note that whether or not your intentions are romantic, to kiss another person on the cheek or elsewhere—or to sniff him or her—it's necessary to move into that individual's "personal space." To get this close, there must be some level of trust or expectation. Thus delivering a friendly kiss or sniff, or receiving one, amounts to an unspoken gesture of acceptance.

What's particularly powerful about the sniffing theory is that we have many accounts of this greeting among indigenous peoples. In 1883, for instance, the British South Seas explorer Alfred St. Johnston published *Camping Among Cannibals*, in which he described how a tribesman in Fiji smelled his hand in a "courteous and respectful" salutation and farewell. Another example comes from Charles Darwin's description of the so-called Malay kiss:

> The women squatted with their faces upturned; my attendants stood leaning over them, laid the bridge of their noses at right angles over theirs and commenced rubbing. It lasted somewhat longer than a hearty hand-shake with us. During this process they uttered a grunt of satisfaction.

Even today, many cultures continue to show affection by smelling a loved one on the cheek. The traditional Canadian Inuit *kunik*, or "Eskimo kiss," does not actually involve rubbing noses together as commonly believed. Instead, it's a kind of nuzzle-sniff. To properly bestow a *kunik*, you press your nostrils against the skin of a loved one and breathe in, thereby suctioning the skin of the recipient against your nose and upper lip. The Maori of New Zealand practice a similar custom.

So might older habits of sniffing really be one reason we kiss today, particularly when it comes to delivering greetings? It's not all that outlandish a possibility when you consider that sampling another person's scent is a primal urge, even if no longer in accordance with polite manners. As we'll see later, laboratory research has found that human subjects report preferring the scent of a partner or their children to that of strangers, suggesting that smell provides important clues into our relationships. As humans developed better language skills, smell probably became less necessary for recognizing one's relatives, but remained an important means to strengthen bonds between people.

Today, of course, blatant sniffing wouldn't generally go over well. It might come across as offensive, embarrassing, or worse. Yet over much of our collective past, sniffing may have been considered a perfectly normal behavior among friends and acquaintances. In fact, it's something many people still do in greeting someone new or entering an unfamiliar home—even though we don't admit it.

As WE HAVE SEEN, there are a great many possible evolutionary pathways that might explain the origins of kissing. The hypotheses I've reviewed may have worked individually to promote kissing, or may have complemented one another and overlapped. But no matter when or where it began, there is little doubt that it was dramatically reinforced once it started.

The work of Rutgers University anthropologist Helen Fisher suggests that kissing's prevalence is ultimately fostered by our brains. She proposes that the behavior likely evolved to facilitate three essential needs: sex drive (*lust*), romantic love (*attraction*), and a sense of calmness and security (*attachment*). Our sex drive encourages us to find partners, romantic love leads us to commit to one person, and attachment keeps us together long enough to have a child. These are not phases, but brain systems that can act together or independently. Each is involved in promoting reproduction, and kissing bolsters all three by encouraging close relationships.

Fisher's reasoning suggests that whatever the *means* by which kissing arrived among us, its persistence can be traced to its advancement of key human social and reproductive needs. With each distinct human culture, it's likely that kissing emerged in part out of instincts rooted in our evolutionary past, but was also influenced by unique social norms among peoples, giving it a very diverse cast in different places.

And humans aren't the only ones exchanging saliva and affectionate gestures, or engaging in kissing and kissing-like behaviors. Many other species were licking, nuzzling, caressing, and more, long before we arrived—and in many ways their behaviors parallel ours, and often seem to serve a similar purpose. The next chapter, then, looks to the animal kingdom for "kissing" among the furry, slimy, prickly, and aquatic creatures with whom we share the planet. From them, we find additional proof that however kissing originated, similar behaviors are shared not only among human cultures but across species—strong evidence that, despite all the variability, affectionate nibbling and muzzling may be rooted in our common evolutionary lineage with the rest of life on earth.

Not All Cues Are Hidden

*I*n 2007, a team of psychologists from the University of New Mexico published a paper suggesting that even though estrus—what we call "being in heat at peak fertility"—is concealed in humans, men may still be able to detect it on a subconscious level. The researchers came up with an ingenious way of studying this by examining the tips earned by eighteen exotic dancers at gentlemen's clubs.

These women recorded the onset of their periods, shift hours, and tip earnings for two months (or some 5,300 lap dances), and the results were intriguing. Dancers earned, on average, $70 per hour when ovulating, $35 per hour while menstruating, and $50 per hour during the weeks in between. Notably, women on birth control pills did not show the earnings peak.

Although the New Mexico scientists aren't entirely sure what to make of this result, and the sample size was limited, it suggests that although modern women do not visually display rosy bottoms, estrus in our own species may not go completely unnoticed. ⇜

CHAPTER 2

Jungle Fever

In the Democratic Republic of Congo, a feisty young male bonobo named Bandaka lived at Lola ya Bonobo Sanctuary. Like many little boys, he enjoyed bullying the girls, and poor Lodja was frequently his victim. Bandaka would pull at her hair and take her toys away, acting like a brute in the sanctuary nursery. The matriarch of their group didn't discipline Bandaka for his bad behavior, so things went on like this for quite a while.

Then in 2006, Bandaka and Lodja were transferred to the adolescent level of the sanctuary. This group's leader forcefully put Bandaka in his place whenever he misbehaved. After one particularly harsh punishment, he fled to the bushes crying while the other bonobos kept their distance. But just then, the most unlikely friend approached: Vanessa Woods watched on as little Lodja wrapped her old enemy in her arms, comforting him with a gentle kiss. The pair spent the rest of the day together as Bandaka groomed Lodja; friends at last.

Bonobo kiss

The heartwarming story of Bandaka and Lodja represents a classic case of kissing behavior that demonstrates the way other animals express affection for similar reasons that we do—not surprising when you consider that humans and bonobos share about 98.7 percent of our DNA.

Bonobos nurse by pouting their lips, much like human infants. Parents have further been observed to kiss-feed their young, and later in life, adults become avid open-mouthed kissers. My favorite example from anthropologist Frans de Waal involves a zookeeper who innocently moved to accept a kiss of greeting from a bonobo and was astonished to feel a second tongue in his mouth!

Just like us, bonobos kiss for a variety of reasons. Known as the most amorous of great apes, they often use sex rather than aggression to resolve conflicts in their female-governed society. They kiss for reassurance, and to firm up their relationships with other members of their community. They have also been observed to kiss after being alarmed or frightened, and often do so to express excitement after there's been clamor in the community. When it comes to kissing, they're among nature's most prolific practitioners: Woods reports seeing bonobos in the Congo kissing and nibbling at each other for up to twelve minutes straight.

And bonobos are just one group of kissers in the animal kingdom. Charles Dickens couldn't have been more wrong when he wrote, "Man is the only animal that knows how to kiss." There are practically as many ways for animals to participate in "kissing" as there are species, and they often do so to express affection, to show submission, to resolve disputes, and more.

However, a caveat is needed here. Behavioral scientists find it extremely difficult to describe the emotional lives of animals other than ourselves. Because different species may process information and interpret the world in vastly diverse ways, it's not really possible for a human to "know" what another animal is feeling and thinking in any meaningful sense of the term. So scientists strive to avoid using words like "love" to describe the animal relationships they observe. Instead, they use terms such as "mate preference" or "selective proceptivity" when explaining the way that other species bond or pair off. Similarly, when it comes to kissing-like behaviors among animals, we cannot assume other species are motivated by the same factors that we are. Yet there is no doubt that they engage in countless affectionate or at times aggressive gestures that closely resemble the human kiss.

Moose and ground squirrels brush noses. Manatees nibble at their partners. Moles rub snouts and turtles tap heads. Porcupines nuzzle noses—one of the few regions of their bodies that lack quills. Voles meet at the face and cats lick one another's heads. Giraffes "neck" by entwining their long necks together, and elephants explore each other's bodies with their trunks. There are even many species of bats that use their tongues during courtship.

These behaviors aren't perfect analogs for the human kiss, but they can serve a similar purpose by bringing two individuals closely together for courtship, bonding, or conflict. These activities among animals take many forms, but they all involve exchanging sensations of taste, smell, and/ or touch, and can serve to define relationships—whether between friends, partners, enemies, family members, or even, in rare cases, members of two separate species.

In fact, we see so many different creatures engaging in kissing-like behaviors that there is probably an adaptive advantage to it all. The process of evolution is driven by reproduction, which in turn is fostered by closeness between the organisms involved. So whether our fellow animals "kiss" to express joy, contentment, love, passion, or confrontation, it is a socially significant means of connecting with another bonobo, dog, or porcupine. These "kisses" lead to a strengthening of bonds, recognition of status, or an act of self-preservation. In the big picture, all of these activities help to perpetuate the species.

So LET'S LOOK MORE closely at some of the most striking and memorable examples of kissing-like behaviors in other species, starting with those most closely related to us and moving out from there.

Just as for humans and bonobos, kissing relieves tension for many other apes as well. Chimpanzees kiss with open mouths but not with their tongues, and primatologist Jane Goodall has reported that they sometimes pout and touch lips in greeting. As with bonobos, chimp kisses can be elicited for many reasons, especially from excitement over the presence of food.

Granted, chimpanzees are not able to experience the same sensations that humans enjoy from kissing because their lips are narrower and do not purse outwardly. Accordingly, they don't kiss in the same contexts that we do; kisses among chimps are probably not a symbol of sexual intimacy, but more an expression of rapport between community members, similar to a human hug. Most observations of chimps kissing involve a quick exchange between females. According to Frans de Waal, kissing among chimps often serves as a way to reestablish bonds and relationships— meaning that humans are not the only ones to "kiss and make up" after quarreling with friends and family members.

But kissing and kissing-like behaviors certainly aren't confined to great apes. Another obvious example occurs in our best friends: dogs. They do much of their social business by means of sniffing at other dogs—a canine parallel to the sniffing greetings that we see in some human societies. Most readers have also no doubt been licked, sometimes in the strangest of nooks and crannies, by a pet dog. Canines lick each other, their owners, and many other people, places, and things. If it's a noun, dogs will probably lick it. It's certainly not a classic "kiss," and not meant romantically or even necessarily as a show of affection. Instead, licking among dogs is a means of greeting and grooming. It can also reflect recognition of social hierarchy, in which subordinates lick more dominant individuals. So the next time it happens to you, consider it a compliment.

Dogs aren't the only lickers; in many animal species, licking is a form of grooming. As animal behaviorist Jonathan Balcombe explains in his book *Pleasurable Kingdom*, scientists have observed that licking can soothe horses, cows, cats, monkeys, and more. These animals' coats protect them from parasites and dirt, so it behooves many same-species pairs to spend hours grooming a partner.

Among mammals, one of the more uncomfortable "kisses" occurs in the elephant seal, a large marine animal that famously features an unusually long and bulbous nose. When an elephant seal wants to mate, he puts his flipper over the side of a female and grips her neck with his teeth. It's not what we would consider the most romantic encounter, but apparently this works for the species. Lions, too, tend to give what can only be described as a rather aggressive "love bite" during sex.

PHOTO: NICOLAS DEVOS

And it's not just our mammal relatives that give kisses or build bonds through behaviors that seem closely related to our own. Many bird species, for instance, nuzzle beaks affectionately (so do dolphins—a different kind of beak, of course). Such "bill-fondling" can appear similar to mammalian or human kissing, as partners caress each other.

It's not surprising that some birds grow so enamored considering that many species, such as parrots and ravens, mate for life. A pair perches side by side, preening and feeding one another. Unlike humans, they can't compose romantic sonnets, so physical affection may serve to express similar sentiments. What's more, pet parrots commonly accept owners as their "mates," and nip tenderly on the lips of their human companion, expressing vulnerability and adoration.

THERE'S ANOTHER SIDE TO "kissing" across the animal kingdom that's not particularly pretty but serves a vital purpose and parallels the process of premastication: regurgitation. Ethologist Niko Tinbergen of Oxford University studied the behavior of herring gulls, in which baby birds peck at the conspicuous red spot on a parent's bright yellow beak as if "kissing" Mom or Dad to be fed. Tinbergen presented chicks with various cardboard gull heads that differed in color, shape, and spot location, hoping to find out exactly what elicited the "kiss" for food. His results revealed that gull chicks are born with a preference for long, yellow objects featuring red spots, providing these young birds with a means of obtaining sustenance right from birth without having to pick up any learning. Regurgitation may sound disgusting, but to baby gulls, getting a parent to spit up is quite literally the "kiss" of life.

Regurgitation for the feeding of young is found among birds ranging from the ibis to the albatross, but some mammals, like wolves, employ a kissing-like behavior to a similar end. Hungry pups nudge and lick the muzzles of adults to stimulate regurgitation and to eat. It may not sound appetizing, but it's effective. Other great apes, cats, dogs, and some marine mammals also feed their young through some form of mouth-to-mouth transmission of food.

And there are still more animal "kissers" out there. A large tropical freshwater fish found in Thailand and Indonesia, called the kissing gourami, touches lips with others, often as a sign of aggression, during feeding, courtship, and fighting. Other species of fish will bite and nudge opponents during combat. Snails, meanwhile, may be the most sensual critters of all, locking together while massaging each other all over.

Even though we will never be able to fully understand the motivations of other species or how they interpret the world, observations of kissing and closely related behaviors suggest that reducing the explanation to mere strategies for survival and reproduction would be far too limited. Additionally, individual animals often exhibit behaviors unique to themselves, not to be found in other members of their particular community. Some press lips, beaks, muzzles, or snouts, while others may express a similar sentiment through a very different display. So in the examples of animal "kissing" provided already, we must not assume that the behaviors recorded are close to 100 percent representative of an entire species. After all, our encounters of animal "kissing" have of necessity been very limited relative to the abundance of life on the planet.

Further, describing many of these unusual, funny, and fascinating styles of "kissing" found in the animal kingdom barely scratches the surface of what's out there, given that scientists estimate there are somewhere between three and thirty million species on earth. What's clear is that evolution is likely behind all of these behaviors, tying individuals together for a wide variety of important reasons.

But if the evidence from the animal kingdom—in combination with the evolutionary accounts we've surveyed— suggests a deep biological basis for kissing-like behaviors, culture is also a central factor in determining precisely what form a kiss takes at a particular time and place. The next two chapters therefore survey the rich pageant of kissing among European and non-European peoples, starting as far back as we can peer toward the dawn of humanity.

In the process, we'll see that humans have gotten pretty good at kissing. Or at least it's clear that our species has had thousands of years to develop, improve, and spread this behavior in its now dominant mouth-to-mouth form.

Koko's Kiss

*K*oko, a female lowland gorilla, was born in 1971, and over her life has been the subject of the longest continuous language experiment ever performed upon a member of a species other than our own. Dr. Penny Patterson has taught Koko over one thousand signs; further, she is capable of understanding around two thousand words of spoken English. Among her extensive vocabulary are the sign and vocalization for "kiss."

When the time came to find Koko a suitable mate, Dr. Patterson showed her video footage of males in zoos, so she would be able to decide which one she wanted to meet. Gorillas like to choose their own partners, so you might say Koko was "video dating." According to researchers, Koko would give a thumbs-up or thumbs-down to each individual depending on whether or not she liked what *she saw—that is, until the moment when a 400-pound male named Ndume from the Brookfield Zoo outside Chicago appeared on the monitor. Koko pressed her lips directly to his image onscreen—leaving scientists with no question as to whom she preferred.* ❧

CHAPTER 3

Kiss My Past

L ooking up at the night sky is like peering back into the past. Here on earth, light travels from one point to another so quickly that it's hard to notice it takes any time at all. But in outer space, distances are so vast that they are measured based on the time period necessary to traverse them. Physicists clock the speed of light at 9,460,730,472,580.8 kilometers per year—very fast, and yet light from the bright stars we see in the night sky still takes a very long time to reach us.

In July 2009, the Hubble Space Telescope captured this image of NGC 6302, otherwise known as the Butterfly Nebula, 3,800 light-years away in the constellation Scorpius:

NGC 6302, the Butterfly Nebula

Perhaps, then, the galaxy's first "kiss" happened a very long time ago, and was made up of star stuff.

Back here on earth, the human lip-print has been traced by classicists and anthropologists over a much shorter period—merely a few millennia. The significance of kissing, its popularity, and its numerous modes have varied dramatically over this time, as have the cultural norms and social expectations of those involved. Many ancient kissing styles would sound and look exceedingly strange to us today. And yet these earlier forms of kissing show many commonalities with what we see in other species, and in our present selves.

If history provides one important lesson with regard to kissing, it's that this behavior is nearly impossible to suppress. Over thousands of years, the kiss has been derided by poets and commentators as disgusting, venal, dirty, and worse. Popes and emperors repeatedly tried to punish practitioners, citing moral or health-related reasons, yet not even the world's most powerful men could police the lips of their subjects. We'll see as much in this chapter as we survey the evidence concerning kissing's cultural origins, significance, and unusual trajectory throughout the ages.

ACCORDING TO SCHOLARS of the relevant historical records, kissing as we know it doesn't seem to make any documented appearance in human societies until around 1500 BC. The earliest and best literary evidence we have for very ancient kissing, according to anthropologist Vaughn Bryant of Texas A&M University, comes from India's Vedic Sanskrit texts, the foundations of the Hindu religion. They began to be compiled in a written form around thirty-five hundred years ago, having previously been part of an oral tradition.

In the Vedic texts no word exists for "kiss," but the same word is employed to mean both "sniff" and "smell," and also has connotations of "touch." Thus when the Atharva-Veda describes a curious act of smelling with the mouth, this could refer to an early kind of sniff-kissing. Similarly, a passage from the Rig-Veda uses the word "sniff/smell" to describe "touching the navel of the world": once again, possibly an ancient kissing reference. Another intriguing line from this text translates to read that a "young lord of the house repeatedly licks the young woman." Here, "lick" may represent a kind of kiss or caress.

By the end of the Vedic period, we get an even more tantalizing clue about early Indian kissing, as the Satapatha Brahmana describes lovers "setting mouth to mouth." An early text of Hindu law, meanwhile, reprimands a man for "drinking the moisture of the lips" of a slave woman. At this point, it appears we are approaching a recognizable description of kissing. And still more evidence appears: The vast Indian epic poem the Mahabharata, which reached its final form in the fourth century BC, describes affectionate kissing on the lips. For example, one line reads, "[She] set her mouth to my mouth and made a noise and that produced pleasure in me."

Latest of all came the famous Vatsyayana Kamasutra, better known as the Kama Sutra. (The word *kama* invokes "pleasure," "desire," "sex," and "love" all at once, while *sutra* roughly means "rules" or "formulas.") This extremely influential sex guide was composed sometime around the third century AD to set rules for pleasure, marriage, and love according to Hindu law, and it details all sorts of sexual behavior, including the kiss. An entire chapter is devoted to the topic of kissing a lover, with instructions on when and where to kiss the body, including "the forehead, the eyes, the cheeks, the throat, the bosom, the breasts, the lips, and the interior of the mouth." The text goes on to describe four methods of kissing—"moderate, contracted, pressed, and soft"—and lays out three kinds of kisses by a young girl or virgin:

NOMINAL KISS: The girl touches lips with her lover but "does not herself do anything."

THROBBING KISS: The girl, "setting aside her bashfulness a little," responds with her lower but not her upper lip.

TOUCHING KISS: The girl "touches her lover's lips with her tongue," closes her eyes, and lays her hands on her lover's hands.

Clearly, people in India were kissing thousands of years ago, but it's doubtful they were the only ones doing so. Consider the Enuma Elish, a Babylonian creation story whose text comes to us from a version recorded on stone tablets in the seventh century BC—though the legends that form its basis are much, much older. The creation story contains reference to several kisses, including a kiss of greeting and a kiss on the ground or feet in supplication.

Much more famously, the Old Testament of the Bible, whose contents are estimated to have been assembled during the twelve centuries before the birth of Christ, abounds with kissing. Notably, in the book of Genesis, the story of Isaac's twin sons Jacob and Esau contains multiple kisses, one of them deceptive.

Esau is the firstborn son and his father's favorite, but Jacob is the clever one. Disguised in his brother's clothes, Jacob comes before the blind and ailing Isaac, who beseeches, "Come near now, and kiss me, my son." Then Isaac sniffs Jacob for recognition, and the deception is complete, for the stolen clothes make his second son smell like Esau, who works outdoors. Isaac proclaims, "See, the smell of my son is as the smell of a field which the LORD hath blessed"—and so Jacob steals his father's blessing from his twin brother, and with it the power to rule.

That's just one of several memorable examples of kissing in the Old Testament. Another comes in the second line of the highly sensual Song of Solomon, which reads, "Let him kiss me with the kisses of his mouth: for thy love is better than wine."

The Greeks, too, have a long and curious history of kissing—one that seems far less focused on romantic or sexual kisses (at least in ancient times) and more on kisses intended to greet or show deference or even supplication. Take the ancient epic the *Odyssey*, composed by Homer (possibly close to three thousand years ago), and finally recorded in writing between the eighth and seventh centuries BC. In it, the hero Odysseus is described as being kissed by his slaves upon his return home as a demonstration of respect—but not on his lips, as they are his inferiors. Another example occurs in the *Iliad*: After Achilles kills Hector, King Priam kisses his enemy's "terrible, man-slaying hands" to plead for the return of his deceased son's body. But we do not find sexual or romantic kissing in Homer.

The *Histories* of Herodotus, written in the fifth century BC, provides an additional cultural catalog of kissing in the classical world. Herodotus relates that among the Persians, where one kissed another person depended on social standing. Equals would greet one another with a kiss on the lips; a slight status inequality between two individuals resulted in a cheek-peck; and if there was a large distinction in the hierarchy, the "lower" person was expected to prostrate himself. (Similar kissing status distinctions were also present in other ancient cultures: Ethiopian kings were kissed on the foot, while Numidian kings were considered too supreme to be kissed at all.) Herodotus also remarked on a sentiment common throughout history: namely, the disdain of kissing certain peoples because of other activities their mouths might engage in. For example, he reported that cow-worshipping Egyptians wouldn't mouth-kiss Greeks, because Greeks consumed their sacred animal.

Around the turn of that century, the Athenian playwright Aristophanes, known for his comedies, had some fun at the expense of kissing. In his works there were kisses entitled the "Spread-outer," the "Weaver," the "Potkiss," the "Doorbolt," the "Limper," the "Doorhinge," and more.

By the fourth century BC, Alexander the Great, the

Greek conqueror and cosmopolitan, stirred up one of the biggest kissing debates of classical times. Among his conquests, Alexander famously incorporated elements of Persian culture into his court, including a type of symbolic kiss called *proskunêsis* that involves paying respect to a superior or monarch by bowing to the ground, and possibly also blowing a kiss. Many Greeks despised the practice, viewing it as the epitome of Eastern despotic decadence.

Moving on to Roman times, and despite our limited records, historians suggest that here developed a strong and vibrant kissing culture—even though some prominent Roman writers and emperors turned up their noses at the practice. Perhaps the strongest Roman kissing proponent was the poet Catullus, as seen in the following famous passage to his love in poem 5:

> Let us live, my Lesbia, and love, and value at one farthing all the talk of crabbed old men. Suns may set and rise again. For us, when the short light has once set, remains to be slept the sleep of one unbroken night. Give me a thousand kisses, then a hundred, then another thousand, then a second hundred, then yet another thousand, then a hundred. Then, when we have made up many thousands, we will confuse our counting, that we may not know the reckoning, nor any malicious person blight them with evil eye, when he knows that our kisses are so many.

The Roman poet Ovid, too, had much to say about kissing, as in his *Ars Amatoria* (*The Art of Love*): "Take heed that when upon her lips you seize / You press them not too hard lest it displease."

By turn-of-the-millennium Rome, members of the populace seem to have been avid mouth-to-mouth kissers. Imperial Rome apparently introduced the practice into other parts of the world via its military—one of the first instances of the kiss being spread along with European culture.

According to classicist Donald Lateiner of Ohio Wesleyan University, historical accounts demonstrate the way Roman men seem to have developed a "mouth fixation," but it's a rare mouth that lived up to their high expectations. For example, in the first century AD, the Roman poet Martial depicted some particularly disgusting kissing encounters in his celebrated *Epigrams*. Here is his account of what happens to an unfortunate man who has returned to Rome after fifteen years:

> Every neighbor, every hairy-faced farmer, presses on you with a strongly-scented kiss. Here the weaver assails you, there the fuller and the cobbler, who has just been kissing leather; here the owner of a filthy beard, and a one-eyed gentleman; there one with bleared eyes, and fellows whose mouths are defiled with all manner of abominations. It was hardly worth the while to return.

Martial wasn't alone; the emperor Tiberius even sought to ban kissing because it helped spread disease. Meanwhile, the Roman statesman Cato advised that when returning home, husbands should kiss their wives—not out of affection but to determine if they had been drinking.

Yet despite the criticisms and jeers, the Romans pressed on orally. They used not one but three different words for kissing, and although their meanings overlap and do not appear to have been perfectly fixed, this is the general breakdown:

OSCULUM: the social or friendship kiss, or kiss out of respect.

BASIUM: the affectionate kiss for family members, also sometimes erotic.

SAVIUM: the sexual or erotic kiss.

There were also several Roman laws on kissing, such as the *osculum interveniens*, which stated that if one member of a betrothed couple died before marriage, whether they had performed this kiss publicly determined how any gifts given between them would be distributed. The kiss demonstrated effectively their status as a committed couple. Afterwards, any gifts received would be split, with half going to the heirs of the deceased.

THERE'S SOME EVIDENCE that one of the most popular kissing traditions we know of today—kissing under the mistletoe—also dates back to the pre-Christian era. In truth, we're not really sure where this custom originated, but there are several possible theories.

In Norse mythology we find the story of Loki, an evil shape-shifting god, who plots to kill Balder, a god of light. All plants and animals, all metals, even fire and water, had vowed to Balder's mother, Frigga, not to hurt her son, with the exception of one plant that was not required to take the oath: the mistletoe. Loki, disguised as a woman, tricks Frigga into revealing this omission. Then he collects the mistletoe, makes it into an arrow or spear, and gives it to Balder's brother Hodr, who fires it at Balder and kills him. This is a great tragedy, but in some versions of the story Balder later arises from the dead, and Frigga forgives the mistletoe and transforms it into a symbol of love, further proclaiming that any two people who walk beneath the plant must kiss.

Another myth comes from the ancient Druids, priests of Celtic Europe who believed the oak tree was sacred. The mistletoe, growing as it did upon the oak, was also a subject of worship. As the Roman writer Pliny recorded:

> The Druids, for so they call their wizards, esteem nothing more sacred than the mistletoe and the tree on which it grows, provided only that the tree is an oak.... The mistletoe is very rarely to be met with; but when it is found, they gather it with solemn ceremony.

The wizards would cut down the mistletoe, which could not be allowed to touch the ground. They believed the plant had near-miraculous powers: as an all-purpose medicine, as a female and animal fertility enhancer, and much more.

A third story comes from the ancient Babylonian-Assyrian empire. Mylitta was their goddess of beauty and love, equivalent to the Greek Aphrodite or Roman Venus. At the Temple of Mylitta, young women would honor the goddess by standing beneath the mistletoe, and were required to give up their bodies and make love to the first man who approached them. It is unclear whether kissing was involved, however, because the custom does not seem to have been common in that era or part of the world.

WITH THE RISE OF CHRISTIANITY, big problems arose for kissing. To put it simply, there was the very valid fear that kissing would lead to other sinful activities of the flesh. Still, the Bible seemed to give kissing quite a lot of license and support in both the Old Testament and the New. Judas's kiss notwithstanding, the apostles were big fans of the practice. Saint Peter referred to the "kiss of charity," and in his Epistle to the Romans Saint Paul wrote, "Salute one another with a holy kiss." Such were the foundations of the "kiss of peace," which became a central part of Catholic church ceremony.

Granted, such biblical exhortations to lock lips could be abused. Priests worried that the "kiss of peace" could serve as an opportunity for kissing among desirous lovers with the apparent blessing of the church. Thus the sexes had to be separated for in-church kissing, and in 397 the third Council of Carthage even sought to ban "religious" kissing between men and women.

But not every kiss during the Middle Ages was a sexy one. Much as Herodotus had described long before, an individual's social standing determined where to kiss another person in greeting. Kisses moved from the lips downward as kissers moved down the social hierarchy. Subjects would kiss the ring and robe of the king, or his hands, or even the ground before him. Similarly, in the church, one kissed the Bible, the priest's robe, or the altar cloth. For the pope, it was proper to press one's lips to his ring or slipper. Catholic priests also started allowing people to kiss illustrations of various saints for a fee known as "kiss money"—just the kind of practice that would later serve as kindling for the Protestant Reformation.

Around this time, a kiss also served as a sign of trust between feudal lords and vassals. Knights would kiss at jousting tournaments, and they would receive a kiss from the person they protected (usually a queen or the wife of a lord) as thanks for a year of service. In fact, a kiss was viewed as an essential mark of gentility, and central to the training of any knight. Of course, as we'll see in part 2, a simple kiss can foster feelings of attachment and more. So not surprisingly, legend has it that the kiss of Lancelot and Guinevere led to the fall of Camelot.

It was also during the Middle Ages that a businesslike kiss was employed as a legal way to seal contracts and business agreements. Many men did not know how to read and write, so they would draw an "X" on the line and kiss it to make it legal. This carried over into the way we write "X" today to symbolize a kiss, as well as the expression "sealed with a kiss." The kiss between a bride and groom was also viewed as marking a kind of legal business agreement, crystallizing all of the responsibilities marriage entailed.

Meanwhile, the church was still wringing its hands about certain kinds of kissing behaviors, and where they might lead. More trouble ensued in the thirteenth century when an English priest came up with an innovation called the osculatorium, also known as the pax-board or simply the pax. It was, in essence, a decorative disk or board made of metal or wood, covered with religious imagery, that could be passed among adherents in church. Members of the congregation would give it a kiss of reverence in lieu of the person-to-person exchange that had marked the "kiss of peace." Alas, the practice of "kissing the disk" created new problems: After a desirable young woman kissed the pax, men would clamor to plant their lips on precisely the same spot. The priests were not happy and sought to prohibit the practice; however, they still accepted kissing for strictly religious reasons if it occurred outside of church.

All the bans and moralizing were only so powerful, though. By 1499, the Dutch humanist scholar Desiderius

Erasmus could write of his travels to England, addressing his friend Faustus, as follows:

> There is a fashion which cannot be commended enough. Wherever you go, you are received on all hands with kisses. If you go back, your salutes are returned to you. When a visit is paid, the first act of hospitality is a kiss, and when guests depart, the same entertainment is repeated; wherever a meeting takes place there is kissing in abundance; in fact whatever way you turn, you are never without it. Oh Faustus, if you had once tasted how sweet and fragrant those kisses are, you would indeed wish to be a traveler, not for ten years, like Solon, but for your whole life, in England.

A notable change came about due to the Great Plague in London around 1665. Kissing understandably lost its popularity, so instead people waved, curtseyed, bowed, or tipped their hats to avoid contracting disease. Still, it appears that social kissing went uninterrupted in seventeenth-century France.

In Germany, meanwhile, a scholar named Martin von Kempe composed an encyclopedia of kisses ambitiously titled the *Opus Polyhistoricum ... de Osculis*, spanning 1,040 pages in length and purporting to exhaust the topic—including a description of over twenty kissing types. In the same era, Germans also came up with categories for lawful and unlawful kisses. For example, women could actually sue men who accosted them with treacherous, lustful, or malicious kisses, although respectful gestures of love and reconciliation were welcome.

By the Industrial Revolution, the hand kiss became popular in England, and eventually evolved into the handshake. At this point in time—as we'll see in the next chapter—kissing had begun to permeate much of the world. The beginnings of globalization integrated people and their social customs across oceans and other natural and man-made boundaries. Where it wasn't already practiced, a European version of kissing would soon arrive thanks to adventurers, tradesmen, and modern technology.

Kiss My Feet

*T*he custom of foot kissing has a long and colorful history, dating at least back to the Babylonian epic of creation. The Roman emperor Caligula had subjects kiss his feet, and this status-oriented kissing was also customary throughout the Middle Ages.

Writing in 1861, Charles Dickens—a huge fan of kissing in general, but also of the little guy—found the practice completely abhorrent, calling it "slavish self-abasement."

Dickens found the foot kissing of the Catholic Church particularly revolting, memorably writing:

> *Valentine the First made the custom permanent; and, ever since 827, the laity has crouched and crawled up to the steps of St. Peter's chair to kiss the toes of the great fetish enshrined thereon. But, as the pope wears a slipper with an embroidered cross upon the upper leathers, by a pleasant fiction saving to pride, men assume that they kiss the sacred symbol and not the human toe: thus adding self-deception to degradation, and committing one unmanliness the more.* 🖎

CHAPTER 4

Cultural Exchange

In his 1864 book *Savage Africa*, the British explorer William Winwood Reade described falling in love with the beautiful daughter of an African king. Reade courted her for months before finally, one evening, daring to give her a kiss. But having never encountered such behavior before, the frightened girl screamed and ran crying from his house. As Reade soon realized, she was terrified of being kissed, thinking it meant he was preparing to eat her.

I've argued up to this point that kissing-like behaviors are part of our evolutionary heritage. But as with all aspects of human and animal behavior, their precise form in a particular place and time is heavily influenced by culture as well. A European-style kiss is certainly not a required intimate activity from a reproductive standpoint, although the behavior is increasingly popular and appears to be spreading. So after surveying the ancient history of the kiss, it is now time to move into our modern world and look at kissing-related behaviors among different peoples, considering how they may relate to our own.

Globalization began with European explorers like Reade, who provided many reports of places where mouth-to-mouth kissing was apparently unknown. Perhaps the most memorable comes from anthropologist Donald Marshall, who studied people living on the Pacific island of Mangaia in what is now known as the Cook Islands. Before Europeans arrived, this culture had not encountered European kissing, but reportedly the men spent their late teens and twenties having an average of twenty-one orgasms a week—making them the most sexually active culture we know. That's over one thousand orgasms a year, apparently without one passionate kiss as we would recognize it.

And it's just one of many similar examples. In another book, 1872's *The Martyrdom of Man*, Reade described a reunion scene he had observed in Africa in which community members greeted hunters who had returned home. Immense affection was displayed, but kissing was absent. Instead, Reade writes, the villagers welcomed the hunters by "murmuring to them in a kind of baby language, calling them by their names of love, shaking their right hands, caressing their faces, patting them upon their breasts, embracing them in all ways except with the lips—for the kiss is unknown among the Africans." Around the same time, travel author and poet Bayard Taylor related similar encounters in a very different part of the world. In

Northern Travel, he noted that some Finnish tribes were not very interested in kissing, and observed that while the sexes would bathe together completely nude, a kiss on the lips was considered indecent. Taylor even met a married Finnish woman and inquired about kissing, to which she replied, "If my husband attempted anything of that kind, I would warm his ears so that he would feel the heat a whole week."

As Europeans continued to document the strange practices of distant peoples, discussions of kissing—or the lack thereof—became a regular feature of texts in the new field of anthropology. Unfortunately, many of these works contain assumptions that would shock us today: European kissing was deemed "civilized" because it was on the lips, whereas one mark of "savages" was their kissing in a more "primitive" or "barbaric" manner—for instance, the sniff kiss. The anthropologist Edward Tylor referred to "the lowest class of salutations" in 1878, observing that they "merge into the civilities which we see exchanged among lower animals." Writing in 1898, the Danish scholar Christopher Nyrop similarly described the European mouth kiss as "a way of salutation vastly superior to the one in vogue among those savage tribes who salute with the nose."

But if we can get past the racism of these texts, they contain fascinating evidence about cultures that seem to have lacked mouth-to-mouth kissing. Nyrop asserted that the practice was unknown in Polynesia, Madagascar, and among some tribes in Africa. Likewise, the anthropologist Alfred E. Crawley wrote in 1929 that kissing on the lips was not to be found in much of the world, outside of the "higher civilizations" like Europe and Greece. More recently, Helen Fisher noted that before contact with Western societies, kissing was "unknown among the Somali, the Lepcha of Sikkim, and the Siriono of South America, whereas the Thonga of South Africa and a few other people tradition- ally found kissing disgusting." The appearance of Western culture is what brought the behavior to their attention, and since then some attitudes have changed. Considering that we also introduced cigarettes and fast-food chains, kissing is probably one of the healthiest customs we've exported around the world.

Mouth-to-mouth kissing may have been present and later disappeared among some cultures for social reasons, such as the discouragement of women's sexuality. But still, Fisher notes that even in societies in which kissing wasn't done, people "patted, licked, rubbed, sucked, nipped, or blew on each other's faces prior to copulation." Indeed, perhaps the most unusual such custom I've come across appears in anthropologist Bronislaw Malinowski's account of lovers in the Trobriand Islands near New Guinea. In 1929, he noted the way inhabitants, among many other strange and sometimes violent sexual behaviors, would bite off one another's eyelashes during intimacy and at orgasm.

"I was never quite able to grasp either the mechanism or the sensuous value of this caress," Malinowski wrote.

But from the perspective of non-European peoples, the idea of mouth-to-mouth kissing must also have seemed very odd—or worse. Among other concerns, the taste and smell of a European kiss was probably pretty unpleasant for those living in cultures that lacked toothbrushes and mouthwash.

Yet kissing as we know it was about to spread. Over time, travel became quicker, easier, and less expensive, while communications technologies created a smaller world than ever before—a process spurred by innovations ranging from the telegraph to the Internet. The result is that today it's estimated that over six billion of us from east to west kiss regularly, lip to lip, as a social and romantic custom.

How did the mouth-to-mouth kiss spread? Many factors were involved beyond the repeated arrival of European ships on new shores. Indeed, perhaps equally powerful were the products of European culture. In the plays of Shakespeare and the novels of Dickens, kissing is a social expectation, and it seems as if everybody does it. We have inherited a legacy of kissing that has been celebrated through art and literature and amplified over time.

In Western culture, many of our most memorable

literary heroes and heroines pass their time waiting for a special kiss to take place. Anticipation moves the story line forward, and the kiss often takes the starring role. It's the happy ending children have come to expect in stories, from *Snow White* to *The Frog Prince*. After all, what would our most celebrated fairy tales be without kissing?

With the advent of the ability to tell narratives visually through film, kissing took on a life of its own. The first onscreen lip-lock was captured in 1896 by the Edison Company, entitled "The May Irwin–John C. Rice Kiss." The entire film lasted less than thirty seconds, and simply consisted of a man and a woman half-kissing, half-talking, followed by a full kiss. They are dressed in formal attire, and Rice sports a rather large mustache. Furthermore, their exchange seems rather perfunctory when compared to today's passionate Hollywood kisses. At the time, however, people were shocked. One review by publisher Herbert S. Stone began, "The spectacle of their prolonged pasturing on each other's lips was hard to bear.... Such things call for police interference." But again, there was no keeping the kiss down—especially not in Hollywood.

Soon silver-screen kisses were everywhere, and not just between men and women. In 1926, *Don Juan* featured the most kisses thus far, a total of 191, provided by John Barrymore to costars Mary Astor and Estelle Taylor, among others. The following year, *Wings* featured the first onscreen male-male kiss on the lips, when a soldier kisses his dying friend. In 1941 came what was reportedly the longest movie kiss at the time, at three minutes and five seconds, between Jane Wyman and Regis Toomey in *You're in the Army Now*. 1961's *Splendor in the Grass*, meanwhile, is credited with featuring Hollywood's first tongue kiss, between Natalie Wood and Warren Beatty. Then in 1963, Andy Warhol released *Kiss*, a fifty-four-minute 16 mm film that consisted solely of kisses between different couples. They lasted about three and a half minutes each (longer than Wyman and Toomey) and the gender of some of the kissers remained ambiguous. Warhol's record was finally broken in 2010 when Tina Fey and Steve Carell kissed for five minutes during the closing credits of the film *Date Night*.

Perhaps what's most extraordinary about this is that much of it took place during the years of the moralistic Motion Picture Production Code, popularly known as the Hays Code, which was in effect from 1930 to 1968. The Code stated that "excessive and lustful kissing, lustful embraces, suggestive postures and gestures, are not to be shown"—the fear being that scenes of passion would "stimulate the lower and baser element." Unless they were essential to the plot, they were not allowed. As a result, a couple's kiss would often culminate in a show of suggestive imagery to hint at what was to come next—burning flames, for instance, or the ringing of wedding bells.

Yet onscreen kissing survived the Hays Code easily enough, and is now a fixture of Hollywood entertainment. Granted, it has not always been without resistance. In 1985, an era characterized by rising concerns about AIDS, the Screen Actors Guild sent out seven thousand letters to agents and producers stipulating that performers should be notified in writing if a film project required them to participate in openmouthed kissing. Such scenes were described as "a possible hazard to the health of actors in light of the lack of clear and consistent medical opinion as to how or in what manner this disease is communicated."

Still, there can be no doubt that due to our cultural products, which carpet the globe, we have done much to teach the rest of the world about our particular form of lip-lock.

HOLLYWOOD CAN'T CONQUER ALL, though. Across latitudes and longitudes today, there's a wide spectrum of what's acceptable and appropriate when it comes to kissing. Each region has distinct tastes and cultural norms, and although it's not possible to trace each one, I'll end this chapter with an admittedly incomplete survey of some common practices from around our increasingly globalized world.

Let's begin in France, home to the "French kiss"—which entered into the English vocabulary in 1923. The precise reason we use this term is unknown, but it's possible that "French kiss" was adopted because American travelers were impressed by the affectionate nature of French women, who were more comfortable with openmouthed kissing than their counterparts. According to anthropologist Vaughn Bryant, this led to a popular saying: "While in France get the girls to kiss you," which later turned into "get a French kiss." In France, it is called a "tongue kiss" or "soul kiss," because if it's done right it's supposed to feel as if two souls are merging.

Cheek kisses in greeting are customary between genders in France and many other parts of the world to express warmth and respect. These kisses are common from Spain to the Netherlands, Portugal to Argentina, in Haiti and Mexico, Switzerland and Belgium, Egypt, Lebanon, and beyond. The salutation usually involves air-kissing one to three times and is typically more the touching of cheeks than lip contact. The appropriate number and direction varies not only by country, but also by community, or even by individual. In many of these regions, men only kiss each other when they are related or close friends, but of course there are exceptions. Elsewhere, cheek kissing among one gender is acceptable, but inappropriate between men and women unless the people are relatives. Such is the case in Turkey and parts of the Middle East.

Elsewhere, public displays of affection are not nearly as popular. Attitudes in Finland haven't completely reversed since the days of Bayard Taylor's visit, where kissing is usually considered a private exchange. Citizens of the United Kingdom are also more likely to nod or shake hands than kiss each other's faces. Likewise, Italians and Germans often save kisses for those with whom they are closest. Yet the German language has thirty words for kissing, including *nachküssen*, meaning a kiss to make up for those that have not occurred. Australians are also more likely to greet friends with a firm handshake than a social kiss. And although friends may sometimes exchange a peck, heterosexual men in that country do not typically kiss each other.

Even though the Kama Sutra was composed in India, kissing there has traditionally been considered a private matter. Most people do not talk about kissing specifically, or their love lives in general, very much. In fact, when Richard Gere spontaneously kissed Bollywood actress Shilpa Shetty in 2007, religious groups held demonstrations in protest and a judge issued an arrest warrant to both of them for violating obscenity laws. In Bahrain and Bangladesh, kisses between parents and children are acceptable, while romantic displays of passion are generally not okay. Likewise, in Thailand, people rarely show affection in public.

In South Africa, a 2008 law forbade people under sixteen from mouth-to-mouth contact in an effort to deal with the high HIV transmission rates in the country. Outraged teens staged kissing protests, and continue to ignore the rule. As noted in the previous chapter, kissing bans never seem to succeed.

In Japan, kissing was traditionally associated with sex.

Therefore, public kissing was considered extremely inappropriate and vulgar for a long time and this kind of behavior was restricted to the privacy of one's home. Indeed, when Rodin's sculpture *The Kiss* was exhibited in the 1920s in Tokyo, it remained shielded behind a bamboo curtain to avoid offending the public. Later, kissing scenes were cut from Hollywood films before they premiered in Japan. But things have loosened up a bit, and today kissing is more acceptable onscreen and—among younger couples—in public.

China has also had a curious relationship with kissing. Twenty years ago, an article in the *Beijing Workers' Daily* advised that the practice was unhealthy and should be discouraged. Generally speaking, compared to Europeans, the Chinese remain much more conservative about kissing. Yet they are growing more open, especially in coastal cities such as Shanghai and Guangzhou. As in Japan, kissing has become increasingly common among young people in China.

Here in the United States, social kissing is not nearly as popular as it is in many parts of Europe. In addition, Americans didn't begin eagerly tongue-kissing until after the First World War—or at least, social factors seemed to influence whether they did it. In Alfred Kinsey's 1948 report *Sexuality in the Human Male*, for instance, kissing style was found to correlate with a person's level of education. Seventy percent of well-educated men admitted to French kissing, while only 40 percent of those who dropped out of high school did. When Kinsey surveyed women five years later he found that those who had experienced premarital sex had a greater incidence of tongue-kissing than those who did not. The findings in his 1953 report also revealed that women placed greater emphasis on kissing than men (a trait we'll return to in chapter 6).

This quick journey barely scratches the surface of global kissing customs and practices, but it's clear social norms vary greatly. Furthermore, bear in mind that we are dealing here in generalizations. Around the globe, we see large individual differences in everything from the way people style their hair to how they prepare dinner. Kissing is no exception, and one person's preference might make another shudder and run, even within the same culture.

Nevertheless, in the modern world kissing is extremely popular—perhaps more than at any other time in human history. We celebrate iconic kissing photographs, like the one between a sailor and a nurse captured by Alfred Eisenstaedt on V-J Day in Times Square that appeared in *Life* magazine. We admire artistic kisses, such as in Gustav Klimt's painting of the same name. We can't forget unexpected kisses, like that shared by Al and Tipper Gore during the 2000 Democratic National Convention. But that's just the beginning. The MTV Video Music Awards memorably featured Michael Jackson kissing Lisa Marie Presley, and later Madonna kissing Britney Spears and Christina Aguilera. Later Sacha Baron Cohen brought us Borat, a character who manages to kiss nearly everyone he encounters—leaving quite an impression on both recipient and audiences.

These moments made headlines around the world with images that will be discussed for decades—perhaps because they are reminders that celebrities, icons, and leaders are not all that different from us. We may vary in skin tone, language, and customs, but in regions around the world kissing has become perhaps the single most universal and humanizing practice that we share.

WITH ALL OF THIS HISTORY, biology, and culture in place, we can now return to the nature-versus-nurture question and ask: What is kissing—genetic or cultural? Clearly, it's more of a compromise than a conflict. Both sides win.

We can always debate just how much a particular behavior with deep biological roots, like kissing, is influenced by our environment or our culture, and which holds greater sway. But in the end, the two must interact—with the result being what gets expressed and acted out. Genes alone are never adequate to account for human or animal behaviors; there are just so many other factors involved.

When it comes to kissing in particular, it's obvious that a slew of social variables shape our attitudes and preferences about what's acceptable and what we like best. Concurrently, kissing or kissing-like behaviors are far too widespread for us to ignore their biological basis. A kiss is certainly much less instinctual than, say, blinking or swallowing, yet the behavior remains etched in our evolutionary history. The experiences we have as we grow affect its human expression and lend kissing a considerable range of variability and diversity—just as they do for so many other species on planet earth.

Kissing Records

*T*he longest kiss on record took place in 2005 between James Belshaw and Sophia Severin at the Plaza Shopping Centre in London. It lasted for 31 hours, 30 minutes, and 30 seconds. The couple didn't sit or sleep, and could only eat and drink through a straw. And as if sipping liquid meals isn't dedication enough, the kiss had to continue through bathroom breaks for it to count.

If you think that's impressive, consider another kissing record. In 2003, Joni Rimm paid $50,000 for the most expensive kiss ever sold at auction. She earned the *privilege of kissing actress Sharon Stone at an AIDS charity event.*

On Valentine's Day 2009 in Mexico City, couples, friends, and family members shared all kinds of kisses for 10 seconds. In total, 39,897 people kissed simultaneously, setting the latest world record. ≋

PART TWO

Kissing

in

the Body

How did it happen that their lips came together? How does it happen that birds sing, that snow melts, that the rose unfolds, that the dawn whitens behind the stark shapes of trees on the quivering summit of the hill? A kiss, and all was said.

—Victor Hugo

CHAPTER 5

The Anatomy of a Kiss

In recent decades, science hasn't just cast light on the likely evolutionary origins of kissing. It has also taught us vastly more about the biology of a kiss as it occurs in our own bodies. By moving on from evolutionary biology and anthropology to physiology, we can start answering the kinds of questions that bear directly on our own romantic experiences: What happens to our bodies during a kiss? And what can we learn from this information about how to do it better?

To begin, let's trace a kiss from the moment of its inception between two partners all the way through the human body, paying close attention to the responses and stimuli that will determine whether we want to continue. I won't distinguish between the male and female kissing experience yet, though obviously it differs greatly—that's the topic of the next chapter. But for now, there's so much to the physiology of a kiss that we'll be busy enough even without introducing a gender divide.

In determining how well a kiss is likely to go over, the environment in which it occurs is the first important factor. For example, the thrill of an erotic kiss, even from the man or woman of your dreams, would probably be greatly tempered during a solemn religious ceremony in a church, synagogue, or mosque (unless that's your kind of thing).

So picture it: The mood is set in a dark, candlelit, romantic setting and the person you adore looks into your eyes, holds you close, and you feel a rush of passion. It seems almost *magical*, and kissing is the first and possibly the only thing on both of your minds.

Even before lips meet, a lot is going on here in the body. In particular, your eyes may be doing something incredible. Psychologist Arthur Aron of the State University of New York at Stony Brook has found that staring into a partner's eyes has a tremendous impact on the feelings associated with falling in love. In his study, Aron paired male and female strangers together for an hour and a half, instructing them to first discuss intimate details of their lives and then, at the end of the time period, to stop talking and stare into one another's eyes for four minutes. Afterwards, many of the research participants reported feeling a deep attraction for the other. In fact, two couples from the study were married within six months.

Let's assume that the eyes and the environment have

done their seductive work and both partners move in for a kiss. Here an important motion happens, although we rarely ever think about it: We tilt our heads, either to the left or right. (Hopefully it's the same way that our partner does coming from the opposite direction, lest there be an awkward collision.)

According to psychologist Onur Güntürkün of the Ruhr-University of Bochum, Germany, about two-thirds of us tilt to the right when we approach for a kiss. In 2003, he reported as much in the journal *Nature* after conducting a rather voyeuristic experiment: Güntürkün watched lovestruck partners, aged roughly thirteen to seventy, kiss in public places like train stations, airports, parks, and beaches in Germany, Turkey, and the United States. To qualify, the kisses under observation required lip contact, a clear head tilt, and a lack of encumbrances, such as bags, luggage, or other objects that might influence the tilt direction.

Interestingly, this tendency toward rightward head tilting does not seem to correlate with the percentage of us who are right-handed, because "righties" are almost eight times more common than "lefties." It has been suggested by Güntürkün that instead, we may adopt our head tilt direction while in utero, as a fetus moves and tilts its head in the womb. However, others expect that the preference is set later in life, as we nurse. Studies show that up to 80 percent of mothers cradle their babies to the left, regardless of whether these moms are left- or right-handed. To nurse, the infants then have to turn their heads to the right, so it's possible many of us learn to associate a rightward head tilt with feelings of affection early in life.

Additionally, there is likely a subtle kind of interactive effect involved in determining a particular kissing alignment. Human gestures help us to interpret speech and understand language, so it's possible that the initiator of a kiss subtly informs the other person about what to do through nonverbal cues. A slight head tilt to the right or left instantly provides visual, tactile, and other sensory signals about the situation. But if head tilt direction gets selected by one partner and shadowed by the other, these respective roles would be nearly impossible for an observer to distinguish. (It is worth noting, however, that following Güntürkün's study, another experiment tested head tilt preference using dolls to eliminate the influence of social cues. The results revealed a similar bias to the right, independent of a partner's influence. So although social clues are undoubtedly involved, other factors are also at work in determining our choice.)

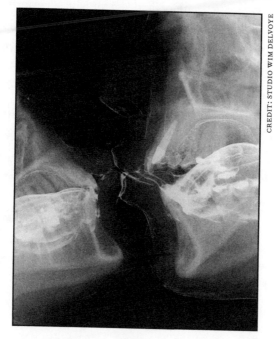

Kiss 4

2000

125 × 100

Cibachrome on aluminium

Even as we're getting our heads aligned for a kiss, we also have to get our mouths ready—which means priming our facial muscles for action. The orbicularis oris muscle runs around the outside of our mouths, making it relatively easy to change the shape of our lips, especially when we're inclined to pucker up. Meanwhile, the zygomaticus major, zygomaticus minor, and levator labii superioris work together to pull up the corners of the mouth and top lip; and the depressor anguli oris and depressor labii inferioris pull down the corners of the mouth and lower lip. And that's just the beginning—an open mouth and tongue movement involves a far more complicated network of facial and postural muscles. Hopefully the recipient is worth all the trouble, as there's significant coordination involved, not to mention the risk of wrinkle lines etched into your face over time from this repeated activity.

But no matter how we get there, eventually—assuming we don't bump foreheads or noses—there's lip contact. That's when things really start to heat up. Five of our twelve cranial nerves switch into high gear. These are the nerves that emerge directly from our brain stem, spreading intricately out to different parts of the face. They are responsible for all sorts of complex activities, helping us to hear, see, smell, taste, touch, and create facial expressions.

During a passionate kiss, our blood vessels dilate and we receive more oxygen than normal to the brain. Our breathing can become irregular and deepen; our cheeks flush, our pulse quickens, and our pupils dilate (which may be one reason that so many of us close our eyes). It's not exactly a workout, but kissing burns a few calories, with the quantity, of course, depending on the kissing session's intensity and length.

A long, openmouthed exchange also allows us to sample

another person's taste. The tongue is ideally designed to gather such information: It is covered with little bumps called papillae that feature our nine to ten thousand taste buds. (Let's hope what they taste is our partner's saliva, and not whatever he or she has been eating.)

And still, that's just a small sample of what's going on. Whether we're relaxed or nervous, our bodies are extremely busy, processing an incredible amount of detail about the situation so we know what to do next.

PERHAPS MOST IMPORTANT OF ALL, when we kiss, all five of our senses are busy transmitting messages to our brain. Billions of little nerve connections are at work, firing away and distributing signals around our bodies. Eventually, these signals reach what is called the somatosensory cortex: the region of the brain that processes feelings of touch, temperature, pain, and more. Here they are interpreted, resulting in "thoughts" such as: "Did he just have onions?" or "Where is that hand wandering?"

The part of our body sending the most information to our brain during a kiss is, without a doubt, the lips. Packed with nerve endings, they are extremely sensitive to pressure, warmth, cold, and indeed to every kind of stimulus. In fact, one of the most remarkable things about the brain's role in kissing is the disproportionate neural space associated with our lips compared with the rest of our body. Just a light brush on them stimulates a very large part of the brain—an area even more expansive than would be activated by sexual stimulation below the belt. This means our lips are our most exposed erogenous zone!

To help get your mind around what this means, take a look at the sculpture below, which has been crafted to reflect the relationship between each part of our body and the proportion of brain tissue dedicated to processing sensory information that comes from it:

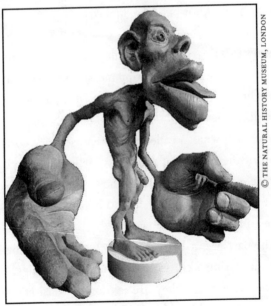

© THE NATURAL HISTORY MUSEUM, LONDON

Sensory homunculus

In this image, the body surface is "mapped" to create a "brain's-eye view." As you can see, the lips and tongue look obscenely large compared with nearly every other feature, because they contain so many sensitive nerve endings. The brain area dedicated to other parts of the body, including the penis, is far smaller in proportion to their sizes. (Although there is not a corresponding sculpture for women, the proportions would be largely the same for most body parts, with the obvious exception of densely innervated organs like the clitoris and breasts. The lips would look enormous in both genders.)

To date, science has barely begun to scratch the surface of the brain's very intricate role in the act of kissing. Far and away the most complex (and mysterious) organ in our body, it is made up of about 100 billion nerve cells, connected at points called synapses and capable of transmitting signals to cells in other parts of the body. These neurons carry a dramatic variety of messages at dazzling speed, a feat they pull off thanks to little molecules called neurotransmitters—the chemical messengers of the brain and nervous system. Neurotransmitters make the leap across synapses between one nerve cell and another, bringing along a particular sort of information with them.

Monkey See, Monkey Do

A contemporary theory in neuroscience involves the possibility of so-called mirror neurons, excitable cells that fire messages in response to someone else's experience as if it were happening to us personally. For example, watching another person get a pinprick on his or her hand would stimulate the same area in our brains as if we ourselves were pricked. It has been speculated that these cells are involved in how we interpret other people's intentions and, therefore, it's possible that mirror neurons may inform us how to respond to being kissed.

In 2003, neuroscientists in Italy attempted to study this phenomenon in macaques, a medium-sized species of monkey. While the researchers did not examine kissing itself, they were interested in the motor neurons responsible for behaviors they termed "lip smacking," "lip protrusion," and "tongue protrusion." They found that about one-third of these cells fired in macaques when they simply observed a human experimenter making one of these kissing-like actions.

If mirror neurons indeed exist, watching another person move forward to kiss us might set off a "kissing response" in our brain as well, encouraging us to shadow the behavior and improving the odds that the kiss will be reciprocated. In the same manner, a partner's excitement during a kiss may serve to increase our own, setting off a feedback loop of mutual anticipation. ⤛

Since it is a strongly sensual experience, a kiss sends sensations directly to the limbic system, those parts of our brain associated with love, passion, and lust. As neural impulses bounce between the brain and the tongue, the facial muscles, the lips, and the skin during kissing, they stimulate our bodies to produce a number of neurotransmitters, and hormones including dopamine, oxytocin, serotonin, and adrenaline. Additionally, the right kiss can lead to the feeling of being on a natural "high" thanks to a rush of endorphins—substances produced by the pituitary gland and the hypothalamus that make us feel exhilarated.

There is much to say about all these chemicals and how they work, but first a general comment. As I mentioned, their job is to transmit different kinds of signals between nerve cells, but while we have some idea as to how they influence our emotions and behaviors, keep in mind that there are legions of them coursing about our brains and bodies at any given time. More than sixty distinct neurotransmitters flow through the body's neural network giving marching orders, in a concoction that has been aptly dubbed the "fluid brain" by endocrinologist Jean-Didier Vincent. So the most important thing to remember is that none of them are acting independently or solely controlling a behavior or experience. Rather, as physicist and science writer Stefan Klein aptly puts it, each neurotransmitter acts as "one voice in a choir." Furthermore, our large cerebral cortex, which is involved in processing thoughts, allows us to make rational decisions that can be at odds with the changes in our bodies—so it is not as though we are entirely "ruled" by chemical signals.

When it comes to kissing, one of the most important neurotransmitters is dopamine, a kind of natural drug associated with the expectation of a reward that brings us feelings of pleasure. Spiking during a passionate kiss, dopamine is responsible for a rush of elation and craving, and can also result in the obsessive thoughts that many of us experience in association with a new romance—almost like an addiction. And no wonder: This neurotransmitter is involved in stimulating the same part of our brain as a line of cocaine. It primes us to want more, making us feel energized. Some people pumping lots of dopamine even lose their appetites, or find that they cannot fall asleep—not surprisingly, the same "symptoms" commonly described when "falling in love."

Fortunately, dopamine does much more than lead to erratic behavior. It also allows us to recognize interesting situations, remember pleasurable experiences, and seek new ones. During the early period of a relationship, novelty triggers a rush of this neurotransmitter, and kissing more than does the trick. With a special person, that first lip contact can literally drug us on feelings of euphoria. Dopamine is probably the reason people say they feel like they are "on cloud nine" or "walking on air." Without a doubt, it's also often to blame for the addictive nature of extramarital affairs. As with many drugs, a person can become dependent on that high, even when he or she feels bad about cheating on a spouse.

But in all relationships, illicit or otherwise, the novelty wears off relatively quickly, and our biology places a limit on how long the "high" conferred by dopamine can last. Studies have shown that levels of this intoxicating neurotransmitter decrease as we become more accustomed to a romantic partner, which might be why sexual desire tends to wane with the same person over time.

Not everyone responds the same way. Humans vary in the number of receptors for dopamine dotting the tips of our nerve cells, and research suggests that a high number may predispose a person to sexual promiscuity or addictive behavior. For instance, geneticist Dean Hamer at the National Institutes of Health has reported a possible correlation between a gene that codes for dopamine receptors and erotic urges in men. Hamer reported that 30 percent of men possess this "promiscuity gene," and they have, on average, 20 percent more sexual partners than average men.

Women can probably experience a similar addiction to sexual novelty due to the increased uptake of dopamine, but the relationship has not been studied in detail (just one example of the way that, until relatively recently, female sexuality has garnered significantly less attention under the scientific microscope). But if a single stretch of genetic material may code for a "wandering eye" in men, the odds are good that it could encourage the same behavior in women.

Granted, dopamine doesn't act independently. It's just part of Klein's "chemical choir," and must share its role with many other neurotransmitters, notably oxytocin, which fosters feelings of attachment and affection and is also associated with kissing. (I will return to oxytocin in chapter 8.) At the same time, a good kiss will also increase the body's level of serotonin, another important chemical involved in regulating our emotions and the transmission of information in the brain. Like dopamine, serotonin can cause obsessive feelings and thoughts about another person. In fact, serotonin levels in someone who reports having just "fallen in love" rival those of patients suffering from obsessive-compulsive disorder (OCD). Meanwhile, a stress hormone called norepinephrine may be responsible for the sensation of feeling weak in the knees.

Finally, the brain sends signals to the adrenal gland to secrete epinephrine (commonly known as adrenaline), boosting our heart rate, making us sweat, reducing stress, and priming our bodies for more physical contact. It also has the potential to distort our perception of a kiss itself. The rush we feel can enhance the experience (or even fool us into pursuing a poorly suited match). But when the mood, the emotions, and the chemical signals are right, a kiss might just be the start of a very intimate evening.

AND WE'RE STILL NOT FINISHED with the brain and kissing, because this incredible organ isn't merely involved in processing sensory data and responding. It's also at work forming memories, and kisses are ideal for that purpose. Psychologist John Bohannon from Butler University has found that most of us can recall up to 90 percent of the details of a first romantic kiss. In his study of five hundred people, most remembered this experience more vividly than their first sexual encounter.

Bohannon's team had expected that the loss of one's virginity would be a more profound memory among study subjects. However, regardless of how much time had passed since a first kiss took place, it left a more indelible mark. Bohannon determined that this memory is so significant that we don't lose it over time, whether it happened six months or twenty-five years ago. Regardless, participants could recall their first kiss in the same amount of detail. He also reported that when both partners are highly aroused during the exchange, they are more likely to remember the same details.

Of course, the power of a kiss isn't limited to its imprint on memory—the sexual impact of lip stimulation can be staggering as well. Alfred Kinsey reported there are some women who can reach orgasm from prolonged deep kissing, even without genital contact.

Now that we've broadly surveyed how a kiss can affect our bodies, it's time to look more closely at particularly important aspects of the human biology involved. The next four chapters explore how the sexes experience kissing differently; the power of smell to turn us on to (or off of) a potential mate after just one kiss; the role of the body's hormones in bringing us all the way from kissing to love; and finally, the germs that make kissing the carrier of at least some small risk beyond matters of the heart.

Kissing Under the Influence

*I*t's not just your driving skills that are affected when you drink or take drugs. Introducing such chemicals into your brain can alter your cognitive and emotional state, and greatly affect your experience of intimate activities as well.

As we've seen, some of the same neurotransmitters associated with kissing can be stimulated through the use of drugs and alcohol—particularly dopamine, which is responsible for feelings of craving and reward. Like a good kiss, they can also stimulate pleasure centers in the brain, making us feel good.

Therefore, mixing a first kiss with these substances can dramatically change your perception of kissing someone—especially critical when it's with a new partner. Intense feelings may be wrongly attributed to the person, when they are really a result of what you have consumed. So the moment your lips connect, you may *experience a rush or even think you're falling in love. And what you mistakenly perceive as a great kiss can quickly lead to getting more physical with altered judgment. But under such circumstances, sobering up can sometimes be a rude awakening when it was in reality the drugs and alcohol rather than the other person that motivated your behavior.* ≋

CHAPTER 6

Women Are from Venus, Men Are Easy

We can't go any further before laying down some gender lines. As with annual medical exams and bicycle seats, men and women have very different needs when it comes to kissing. And a quick browse of the Internet provides a glimpse of how confused we often are regarding the desires of the opposite sex in this area. For instance, some current kissing advice at MensHealth.com reads:

> Suck on her tongue mimicking the way you would suck on her clitoris. She'll catch on quite quickly and perhaps after that you can let her suck on your finger so that she can return the favor.

In the writer's defense, openmouthed kissing and cunnilingus are often associated across cultures—the Latin word for lips is *labia*, after all. But while the above technique *may* work out occasionally for a particularly charismatic gentleman, the novice attempting to impress an unsuspecting crush with this move might not fare as well. Suffice it to say that to the average inexperienced suitor approaching first base, I strongly caution against taking such instructions literally.

Women are not much better off in terms of the advice we receive. In fact, we may be even more confused, and websites geared toward us provide equally amusing—if not misguided—tips. As this book was being written, for instance, iVillage.com featured a piece called "Kiss Your Way to Better Sex," which offered instructions to "guide him to better kissing." Here's a sample:

> To tweak his [kissing] style, it's important that you use one-word directions, such as "lighter," "left," "right," etc.

Sure, this advice might be helpful for some openly communicative couples. But it could also come across as awkward, if not intimidating, to many men—especially given that a comfortable environment is very important for a kiss to go well.

I'm not suggesting that we should always ignore the kissing tips provided by pop gurus, but these examples illustrate the way men and women are often thinking about very different aspects of the encounter. Science can help us understand why. Although kissing can serve many purposes, it is part of human sexual behavior, an area where men and women have distinct motivations. Mars and Venus, as John Gray termed it, with the data to boot.

In a recent survey published in the journal *Evolutionary Psychology*, for instance, researchers from the State University of New York at Albany asked 1,041 heterosexual college undergrads about their kissing preferences. To make sure the responses were based on firsthand experience, the study excluded those who reported never having romantically kissed another person.

The scientists were interested to learn how kissing is involved in helping us choose a partner and bond with him or her, and how it impacts sexual arousal and receptivity. Their results were extremely enlightening, as a dramatic gender divide emerged. For example, only one in seven women answered that she would consider sex with someone she had not first kissed. Conversely, the majority of men reported that they would not be deterred.

That was just the beginning. Women were far more likely to see kissing as a good way to assess a potential mate or to initiate, maintain, and monitor a long-term relationship. They also rated the breath and taste of a man's kiss as highly significant in determining whether to keep on kissing him in the moment or the future. Women were far more interested in healthy-looking teeth, and reported valuing the experience of kissing much more than men did—before, during, and after a sexual encounter.

Men, on the other hand, were much less picky about

kissing and far more interested in facial and bodily attractiveness. For them, "finding a good kisser" might be enough of a reason to begin a relationship, and they were also more likely to kiss someone whom they knew "only wanted to have sex." Overall, men placed less importance on kissing in their relationships, regardless of how long they'd been dating someone. Finally, the survey revealed that men were a lot more likely to have sex with a person they considered to be a bad kisser.

Clearly, the women in this experiment appear to value kissing itself much more than men, and treat it as a kind of litmus test for weighing the status of a relationship. Meanwhile, men do not appear to be as focused on deciphering the significance of the exchange and tend to think of it as a way to induce arousal or to pick up on cues about a woman's sexual receptiveness. (There are even studies of date rapists finding that men generally feel more entitled to force sex with a woman after they have been kissing.)

What's more, the differences observed by the Albany psychologists are not limited to Americans. Behavioral scientists have obtained similar results in other parts of the world, too. Psychologists Marita McCabe and John Collins at Macquarie University in Australia surveyed men and women about their desires during the early stages of a new relationship. They found that men more frequently expressed the desire to touch a partner's breasts and genitals, while women often wanted sensual kissing and physical contact.

Does all of this simply confirm what reality television and prime-time sitcoms have suggested all along—that most men spend their lives doing whatever it takes to "get lucky"? Not exactly. But it's clear that they place less significance on the act of kissing, particularly with a short-term partner. For them, kissing seems more a means to an end: They swap spit in the hopes of swapping other bodily fluids later. Thus, while the websites I perused may have failed to impart good kissing advice to readers, they probably did appeal to the interests and assumptions of their intended audiences.

AT AROUND THIS POINT in my research on the difference in responses to kissing based on gender, I started getting pretty frustrated. I'm no fan of clichés about the sexes, as they can often be meaningless generalizations.

What's more, I was somewhat skeptical of the results of the studies described above, and wanted to prove that men and women are less predictable than such findings suggest. Just consider some possible flaws. The *Evolutionary Psychology* study only examined college students—a time in men's lives when they are chock-full of testosterone, wanderlust, and who knows what else. Similarly, the women surveyed were probably getting tired of hanging around these men and enduring their constant advances. The dormitory lifestyle is hardly reflective of how the general public lives, and what's more, the researchers' methods only considered heterosexual subjects. I expected that my colleagues and acquaintances wouldn't provide such polarized responses, reasoning that their lives and perspectives would be far more diverse and unpredictable than those of the student volunteers.

So I conducted my own informal survey, asking eighty schoolteachers, writers, stay-at-home-moms, scientists, construction workers, salespeople, professors, attorneys, students, and retired businesspeople about their attitudes on kissing based on the original survey questions. The group included forty-two women and thirty-eight men. Since these were people I knew personally, my "poll" was not random and could not be considered truly scientific in nature, but the subjects ranged in age from eighteen to eighty and included hetero-, homo-, and bisexual respondents. They had been raised in many different parts of the world, and ran the gamut when it came to relationship status: single, married, divorced, remarried, widowed, and "it's complicated."

I hoped to blow some gender expectations out of the water.

Then came a big surprise: I *couldn't*. The general trends, as reported in the original *Evolutionary Psychology* survey, held up perfectly in my own informal questionnaire, despite the very different set of people I'd questioned. Most men admitted to being eager to engage in sexual activities with or without a kiss, whereas several women actually called or emailed asking why they'd even be in that situation in the first place. Only three women (about 7 percent) said they would even consider it, while two asked if the question subtly implied prostitution.

As far as I could tell, my friends might as well be the college coeds. With my hopes of shattering gender stereotypes dashed, I had no other choice: I called up an author on the original "kissing attitudes" study, evolutionary psychologist Gordon Gallup Jr. of the State University of New York at Albany, to help me grapple with the results.

Gallup patiently explained that attitudes on kissing are more complex than they may appear based on a cursory reading of his study. Surveys by evolutionary psychologists certainly do report that women tend to place more emphasis on the kiss itself, but to my relief, he emphasized that kissing does matter to men too—just in different ways.

Biologically, men can be less picky about kissing because, unlike women, they are capable of spreading millions of sperm around. Men produce loads of the stuff, constantly. Each sperm is like a DNA-packed missile, armed with twenty-three chromosomes and programmed to find and storm its target upon launch. It's a microscopic powerhouse of energy with a single mission: to outpace tens of millions of competitors and fuse with a woman's egg, creating a new forty-six-chromosomed human being.

Barring illness or medical problems, the amount of sperm a single man can produce in his lifetime is virtually unlimited. With a lot of determination and stamina, he could theoretically impregnate hundreds, if not thousands, of women. Biology doesn't require him to carry a developing baby for nine months to term or to nurse, care for, or even necessarily provide it with resources (although in our modern society, the law generally does). From a strictly wham-bam-thank-you-ma'am perspective, a man can be off to the next conquest in minutes.

Consider the famous thirteenth-century rapist and plunderer Genghis Khan. He not only had sexual access to six Mongolian wives and many daughters of foreign kings whose lands he conquered, he also raped countless women as he ravaged China and neighboring lands. The most beautiful young women from looted villages were delivered to Khan for forced sexual intercourse—a brutal act that resulted in many, many children. This man was so reproductively successful that geneticists have discovered his DNA lives on today in an estimated sixteen million men living in Asia, from Manchuria to Uzbekistan to Afghanistan. So a single man who lived nearly one thousand years ago may be a direct ancestor of every one in two hundred men living on earth today.

If limitless sperm isn't reason enough for men to approach sexual relationships casually—without a huge emphasis on the importance of kissing as a way of identifying the perfect partner—men also have another big advantage over women: time. They can continue to inseminate fertile women over many, many decades. For example, in 2007, a farmer in India named Nanu Ram Jogi had his twenty-first child at age ninety by his fourth wife. And according to interviews, he hopes for more.

Regardless of how far women have come in recent

decades, there are still some areas where we can't presume to compete. We are biologically different from men, and even the most devoted fathers are physically unable to make an equal parental investment in their offspring. When it comes to mating and reproduction, women physically bear much more responsibility—and also have a lot less opportunity, despite modern advances in medicine.

We are quite literally born with all of our eggs in two baskets—our ovaries. Baby girls arrive on planet earth with one to two million immature eggs called follicles, but the majority die off early. When puberty hits, we have, on average, about 400,000 such follicles left. Then we shed one developed ovum—along with about one thousand follicles—every time we ovulate. In the end, only about four hundred of the original follicles ever reach maturity, giving us, on average, about thirty-three years of fertility before menopause. And while we are still ovulating, each ovum has just five or six days during which it might get fertilized before being shed through menstruation.

Thus, when it comes to the chance of passing along our genes, life isn't exactly fair. Four hundred mature eggs versus limitless sperm does not provide an equal playing field. Yet women do have one extremely significant advantage that makes all the difference in the mating game: Barring cases of surrogacy, a woman always knows for certain that the baby she bears carries her genetic information. By contrast, at least until recent technological innovations in

DNA analysis, men could never be so sure. Consider: In the United States, of those men who opt to take paternity tests, 30 percent find out they are not the child's father. (It is important to note that the men who want to be tested likely have reason to be suspicious of their paternity in the first place, so this figure is probably skewed toward the high end and not representative of the general population.)

Clearly, women have a vested interest in choosing a father who's going to stick around and help raise a child. To that end, we need ways—like kissing—to assess if someone has "good genes," and whether he's healthy, to ensure that our offspring will have the best possible start in life. When we meet that partner at the lips, then, we have lots of work to do. We are actively interpreting all sorts of critical information about him. If a match is doomed—genetically, behaviorally, or otherwise—it behooves a woman with an aging and limited egg supply to know as soon as possible. She benefits by leaving while there is still optimal opportunity to reproduce with someone else.

A look at divorce statistics around the world reflects this reality. In another study, Gallup and his colleagues examined 1.7 million global breakups, and found some thought-provoking trends. In married couples aged twenty and younger, a whopping 99 percent of the time, the woman is the person who files for divorce. Those are some very young couples, but it turns out that females are more likely to initiate divorce up through age sixty-five, although the likelihood decreases as we age. On some level, women seem to "know" that if things are not going right during our most reproductive years, we're better off getting out early.

In our interview, Gallup further explained that particularly for women, a kiss probably serves as a very early indicator on whether to pursue a union at all—a quick test of compatibility. Rather than a relationship making it all the way to a divorce petition, a kiss can sometimes halt a star-crossed couple before they get started, which is why the first kiss can be so critical. A woman who doesn't like the experience is probably "learning" that she is not very compatible with her partner as her body lets her "know" not to invest time and energy in this person. Conversely, a kiss that feels and tastes good fosters positive sensations, motivating her to pursue a deeper connection.

How does she "know" whether she is kissing the right man? That's what we'll learn in the next chapter. Because kissing involves the exchange of so much information through body chemistry, smell, and touch, humans have probably evolved ways to use it all to help determine whether moving forward with someone is in our best interest. Subconsciously, both partners are picking up on clues about the other's health, reproductive potential, and even whether their very genetic codes may be compatible.

For now, though, there's just no way around it: Men and women approach kissing with very different expectations, attitudes, and preferences. But take heart, it's still enjoyable for most everyone. A 2003 survey of 295 college students at Brigham Young University found that respondents ranked kissing on the lips higher than massages, hugging, caressing, cuddling, holding hands, and kissing the face. While this study was conducted at a Mormon school with serious restrictions on sexual contact between genders, the conclusion is likely near-universal. Overall, the researchers showed that the amount a couple kissed was proportional to their stated level of relationship satisfaction.

So it's certainly true: Evolutionarily speaking, men may be less picky about a partner than women. But Mars and Venus can each still value kissing. What's more, members of both sexes can get *better* at it, whatever their goals—and both have strong motivations to so do. The sexes may view the kiss differently, but in the end, let's not forget: The kiss also brings them *together*.

The Coolidge Effect

*A*s we've seen in chapter 5, *dopamine spikes due to novel experiences. This is likely involved in the phenomenon known as the "Coolidge effect": the scientific name for the decline of sexual attraction in relationships over time.*

The Coolidge effect gets its name from a memorable

anecdote that supposedly took place during Calvin Coolidge's presidency (1923–29). As the story goes, First Lady Grace Coolidge entered a government farm's chicken coop while a rooster was mounting a hen. She was told the cock copulated dozens of times a day, and reportedly responded, "Go tell that to the president." When her husband was informed of the bird's sexual exploits, he asked whether each rooster routinely serviced the same hen. Upon learning there are many females for each rooster, it's said that the president replied, "Tell that to Mrs. Coolidge." ⤚

CHAPTER 7

Scent of a Man

In the 1985 film *Back to the Future*, Marty McFly travels thirty years into the past and encounters his parents as teenagers. After mistakenly thwarting the moment when they are first supposed to meet, he is horrified to find that his mother, Lorraine, falls for him instead of his dad. So Marty plots a convoluted scheme to reunite them by taking Lorraine to the high school dance, but as they sit parked in a car she instead grabs him, her son, for a kiss. Fortunately, in that moment Lorraine's romantic feelings for Marty instantly change. "This is all wrong," she says. "I don't know what it is, but when I'm kissing you, it's like I'm kissing my brother."

Offscreen as well as on, it's not at all uncommon to kiss someone seemingly perfect, only to discover you're no longer interested in romance once your lips meet. Up until then, the stars seemed perfectly aligned for embarking on a great relationship, but afterward you instinctively sense something's not right. The first kiss is a necessary risk in every budding sexual relationship; a recent psychology study found that 59 percent of men and 66 percent of women reported breaking things off with a prospective partner because of it.

How can a seemingly simple exchange trigger such a dramatic reversal? As it turns out, our sense of smell may be responsible, along with some very important genes and, perhaps most controversially, chemical messengers called pheromones. When it comes to deciding whether to pursue relationships in the earliest stages, your nose could serve as the ultimate mood killer.

Smell is a form of what scientists call "chemoreception"—a natural way to recognize chemical information from our environment so as to learn more about particular situations. For a long time, science sold this sense short, assuming that people had relatively poor olfactory abilities compared to other animals. The evidence from human evolution seemed to support the assumption: Standing upright moved our ancestors' noses away from the aromatic ground, and we accordingly developed smaller "snouts" than other species of primates. Geneticists have also determined that, compared with our nonhuman ancestors, we have fewer genes devoted to detecting scent.

But that doesn't mean our sense of smell should be overlooked. In 2004, Yale neuroscientist Gordon Shepherd surveyed the research on human olfaction and concluded that it is probably more important than usually acknowledged.

Indeed, Shepherd reported, our nasal cavities, brains, and language abilities allow us to analyze smell in a more comprehensive way than other animals do.

Not surprisingly, odor plays a key role when we are sharing close quarters with another person. Ancient Roman poets, for example, described kisses that smelled of fresh flowers and incense. While this surely indulges in a bit of artistic license, there's no doubt that a person's odor can have a strong effect upon those they encounter, working either as an attractant or a repellant.

When it comes to kissing, factors like poor hygiene and bad breath can certainly spoil a promising moment, but it's often our body's natural scent that makes the most powerful impression. All over the world, people describe the smells of their lovers, spouses, children, and friends as pleasant, while they often remember the odors of strangers in the opposite way. How could this be? To understand what's going on, we need to explore the body's top sources of natural scent, known as the sebaceous and apocrine glands.

Sebaceous glands are found in the skin throughout our bodies, but are most highly concentrated around the nose and on our necks and faces. These glands secrete an oily substance called sebum, which contains our unique scent. When we reach puberty, the flow of sebum increases and our personal odor becomes more pronounced. Humans are very sensitive to this musk, and perhaps never more so than when kissing, with our noses often directly pressed against another's skin.

High concentrations of an individual's scent are also released through the apocrine glands, which can be found at the intersection of the skin and the fat stored just below. They occur throughout the body, but are heavily concentrated in the armpits and genital region where hair tufts grow, serving as a kind of scent trap. These glands also become more pronounced during puberty and release small secretions, which then dissolve into our sweat and spread. As the solution mixes with bacteria it becomes pungent, leading scientists to dub the entire underarm region the "axillary scent organ." Interestingly, people from some regions, such as East Asia, often have fewer apocrine glands than those from others, like Europe and Africa.

The axillary organ is unique to humans and other apes, suggesting it evolved relatively recently. Anthropologists have long assumed it plays a strong role in producing an enticing scent to allure members of the opposite gender. Granted, what was enticing many thousands of years ago is not necessarily so today—but there's much evidence from more recent history about the power of axillary scents and their role in relationships and sex.

In 1840, the English physician Thomas Laycock called the axillary odor "musky...certainly the sexual odour of man." By the early 1900s scientists were describing the odors emanating from both sexes as attractants. In 1975, psychologist Benjamin Brody reported a practice in rural

Austria in which girls would dance with an apple slice in their armpits and afterward would give it to the most worthy gentleman. In turn, he would politely, perhaps even gladly, gobble it up. It's an unusual means of courtship, but if our body secretions are as powerful as science suggests, it was probably an effective custom.

In 1977 Austrian ethologist Irenäus Eibl-Eibesfeldt described a kind of ceremonial farewell among members of the Gidjingali tribe in Australia. A man would wipe his hands through his own underarms and then those of his departing friend. Next he would touch each of their chests. Although this sounds strange to us, it demonstrates the way that body odors have played an important role in maintaining human social bonds around the world.

Apocrine glands are larger in men, and each sex harbors a different bacterial community, giving men and women distinct scents. While the genital region seems an obvious place for the location of these glands, scientists aren't sure about why they also exist in our underarms. Zoologist Desmond Morris memorably suggested that the axillary scent may serve to stimulate a partner during face-to-face sex, when each participant's head is in close quarters with the other's armpits—but that has yet to be supported by research.

Still, there are reasons to think the smells emitted by the apocrine and sebaceous glands may have the power to start or end a relationship. A central role in the process could hinge on the first kiss, which brings two people into their closest proximity yet and so serves as a kind of preliminary evaluation—and sometimes even involves swapping some sebum along with our saliva.

BUT IT'S NOT JUST our conscious reaction to another person's smell that counts. Olfaction may also help us, on an unconscious level, to evaluate our genetic compatibility with a potential sexual partner.

For a long time, scientists have known that humans display our genetic fitness to the opposite sex through certain physical attributes. For example, many studies have shown that we're most attracted to people with very symmetrical facial features, subconsciously recognizing these to be an indicator of health and "good" genes. Similarly, a square jaw is considered "manly" because it's a visible display of testosterone, while a narrow waist and wide hips in women signify reproductive capacity. In these examples, physical traits have become valued or associated with "beauty" in some cultures because they are able to provide information about the status of another person's health, age, and fertility.

But there is probably far more to the subconscious evaluation of a partner's genetic fitness than what we see. Sight is only one out of five senses, after all. Much research suggests that smell also helps us detect suitable partners, in a sense allowing us to sniff their very genes.

One of the most heavily discussed topics in human mate selection is the major histocompatibility complex (MHC), a group of genes that control how our immune system defends itself against disease. The MHC genes contain the DNA recipe for a certain set of proteins located on the outer surfaces of our cells, whose job is to tell the difference between cells from the body's home team and bacteria, viruses, or fungi. When a person carries more variation in MHC genes, his or her body has an easier time recognizing these foreign invaders.

MHC diversity is also very important for producing offspring with flexible and versatile immune systems. Children benefit most when they have distinct MHC genetic material from their parents. This makes detecting MHC variation in a partner very important for the health and survival of the next generation.

But how do we identify potential romantic partners with a distinctly different MHC? We certainly aren't sequencing their DNA. Rather, the most powerful signals may be conveyed through their natural scent.

Consider the famous 1995 "sweaty T-shirt experiment," in which Swiss zoologist Claus Wedekind studied women's sensitivities to male odors. He selected forty-nine women and forty-four men after testing their DNA to determine each person's MHC type. The men wore clean T-shirts without deodorant for two nights and then returned them to Wedekind. Next, his team placed each shirt in a box with a smelling hole. The women sampled the odor of seven boxes and described each based on its pleasantness, sexiness, and odorous intensity.

The results were striking: Women nearly always preferred the scents of T-shirts worn by men with MHC genes different from their own—suggesting that we can determine our genetic compatibility with potential partners simply by following our noses. This may be particularly the case for women, who have more powerful senses of smell and taste than men, additionally heightened during peak fertility.

Many subsequent studies have been conducted since the original "sweaty T-shirt experiment," yielding similar results. In this additional research, test subjects have also been found to rank the clothes worn by their partners and children as the most pleasant-smelling. One particularly intriguing result came from a 2006 study conducted at the University of New Mexico, which considered the MHC genes and bedroom behavior of forty-eight couples. The researchers found that the women who were more genetically distinct from their partners reported a higher degree of sexual satisfaction. Those with similar MHC genes, by contrast, reported having more fantasies about other men, and were also more likely to cheat.

Scientists have since published many articles suggesting that the odors we tend to favor emanate from those with very different immune systems from our own. However, there's one big and notable exception: Women on the birth control pill display the opposite response. Rather than feeling most attracted to the scent of genetically distinct men, they are more likely to prefer those with very similar MHC genes to their own.

Scientists are not entirely sure why this effect occurs, but one interesting (though highly speculative) theory suggests it may have to do with the way the pill works. Birth control hormones typically fool a woman's body into thinking that she is pregnant. An expectant mother would no longer need to seek a suitable genetic partner after fertilization has taken place. Instead, it would normally be in her best interest to stay close to her own family and those who are most likely to take care of her and her children. That means parents, siblings, and cousins—those who probably have the most similar genes, and scents—could have the most appealing odors to her during pregnancy. Thus it's possible that women using birth control might be most attracted to the scents of men who are less than ideal genetic matches when it comes to reproduction.

If true, it's possible that going on or off the pill during a relationship may alter a woman's perceived level of attraction to the person she is with. It has even been suggested that this transition could be related to divorce rates in young couples. When a woman goes off the pill when she and her husband want to have a baby, their romantic chemistry may suffer, straining the relationship.

However, while this is an intriguing possibility, it's

unclear how significant the MHC is when women choose a partner. Furthermore, many complex factors besides genetics are at work keeping successful couples together or pushing unsuccessful ones apart. At present, the relationship between MHC genes and sexual attraction continues to be explored and debated. For instance, some research suggests that there is an MHC-related odor preference in both sexes, while other studies find that it mainly affects women. So while there seems to be some type of correlation between our immunity genes and our preferences in choosing a partner, science probably should not oversell it, especially when so little of the human genome is understood.

One geneticist I interviewed put it like this: Looking for the key to human relationship chemistry in a single region of our vast genome, like the MHC, is somewhat analogous to a drunk searching for his car keys under a streetlight. If we're expecting to find answers in one particular spot of the genetic code, perhaps that's just because it's one of the few illuminated areas where we know to look.

Still, there's probably something in the poet William Cowper's remark that "Variety's the very spice of life, that gives it all its flavor." In genetic terms, detecting such variety requires very close proximity to a partner—a crossing of the social and cultural boundaries that delineate "personal space." A kiss is one of the few ways to bridge that gap in a mutually acceptable, nonthreatening way. In this manner, kissing may serve as our genetic guide.

• • •

AND THERE'S AN EVEN more scientifically controversial theory about the way in which our bodies could be picking up information about the suitability of our partners. In 1959, German biochemist Peter Karlson and Swiss entomologist Martin Lüscher introduced science to the term "pheromone," which means "carrier of excitement" in Greek. Karlson and Lüscher used the word to describe a substance released by an animal in order to trigger a behavioral or developmental reaction in another individual of the same species. While this definition works very well for insects like moths and termites—known to depend on pheromones for attracting mates, locating food, and signaling alarm— understanding its applicability is far more complex in vertebrates like ourselves.

Take laboratory mice, for example. We know they have an ability to detect pheromones, and that they release many of them in their urine. Nevertheless, scientists have struggled to determine which components of this mixture are responsible for a particular behavior in another mouse. A mouse's urine concoction contains hundreds of different organic compounds, and an individual's response to them might be influenced by many factors outside of chemistry, such as fear or curiosity. So even when we know pheromones are at work, it can be challenging to weed out a causal relationship between a particular chemical and a specific behavioral response.

In other cases, though, it's much easier to catch pheromones in action. Take pigs, which have a vomeronasal organ (VNO) located between their nose and mouth that senses these odorless chemicals. Male pigs produce a chemical called androstenone in their saliva, and when females of the species detect it, they go into a rigid stance and prepare to be mounted—a pretty clear-cut cause-and-effect example of pheromones at work. In fact, androstenone elicits such a powerful response that pig farmers use a commercially produced version to determine when sows are ready for insemination.

While many men would surely love to carry a version of that pheromone around in a bottle—and indeed, several perfume companies claim to have one on sale—scientists say we're not there yet. In fact, the experts cannot even decide whether humans have the ability to detect pheromones at all. At least for the present, the evidence on the subject is spotty and controversial—but some of it is pretty intriguing as well.

Consider, for instance, the tendency for women who spend a lot of time together to develop synchronized menstrual cycles. It's not folklore, there have been many scientific investigations on the matter. In 1971, psychologist Martha McClintock performed the first such research at Wellesley College, interviewing 137 women living in an all-female dormitory. McClintock recorded data about the date of onset for each woman's period and then compared it to those of her roommates and friends. Her results, published in the journal *Nature*, showed that the time between menstrual onset decreased for women who spent the most time together. Because of this work, menstrual synchrony is now also known as the "McClintock effect."

Since then, much additional research has examined how women may influence one another's menstrual cycles, and some even debate whether such synchronization happens at all. Still, I expect that many women reading this have probably witnessed the McClintock effect firsthand, and a good deal of research published since the *Nature* article first appeared supports the original findings. While scientists do not know exactly why the effect happens, pheromones are the most common guess.

More recently, research has demonstrated that when women are ovulating, male partners tend to be more attentive, affectionate, and romantic than on average. And as it happens, they are also more likely to be jealous of other men during this period. Scientists have proposed several triggers for this behavior, which are not mutually exclusive and probably serve to reinforce one another.

For example, at peak fertility, a woman's mood and behavior often reflect her increased interest in sex. She is more likely to be attracted to dominant masculine features like a square jaw, to pay greater attention to the way she dresses, and to go out to social functions. There is also research suggesting she may have an enhanced likelihood of cheating on her partner. So it's possible the man in her life will be responding to her change in behavior. However, pheromones may also be at work, sending him subtle signals about her body's reproductive status and fostering the urge to care for and protect his partner.

Studies also suggest that a reason for enhanced libido may be that during ovulation, women become increasingly sensitive to androstenone, a chemical in human male sweat (the same one that's in pigs). In the famous 1980 "dentist's chair experiment," for instance, androstenone was sprayed on a chair in a dentist's waiting room, and scientists then observed where test subjects chose to sit. They noted that women tended to sit in the pheromone-covered chair, whereas men avoided it. In another study, the same pheromone was applied to a specific restroom stall, and once again, men avoided the treated door. When women were tested in that scenario, however, they did not seem to exhibit any obvious preference.

Some have proposed a possible relationship between the amount of androstenone secreted by men and the levels of the sex hormone testosterone in their bodies. If it exists, then perhaps during a woman's most fertile time of the month, she can detect silent signals that draw her to men who are pumping the most testosterone. Kissing them would then put her in close proximity to all that male sweat and androstenone—which would further increase her arousal and receptivity to sex.

Another human pheromone suspect is androstadienone, also found in male sweat, and also involved with testosterone. This chemical has been reported to influence the mood of heterosexual women, making them feel more relaxed. Meanwhile, about one-third of women also release substances called copulins in their vaginal secretions. Some studies suggest these compounds may work to increase libido and raise testosterone levels in male partners, which would make them pheromones, but scientists still aren't sure how strong an influence they may have.

Still, there's a huge problem with all this human pheromone talk. For while scientists have identified substances secreted by both men and women that *may* act as pheromones, it's unclear whether we even have a special organ to detect them. Researchers have suggested that humans, too, might have a kind of VNO. Small holes just inside our nasal opening, on either side of the septum, have been observed in many individuals, varying in size, shape, and location for each person. However, the cells in this region of the body do not appear to connect with the nerves that would presumably be necessary to transmit pheromonal information.

And there are other reasons for hedging. The current near-consensus of scientists studying pheromones is that a single chemical compound cannot ensure a specific response under every circumstance. Many hormonal and physiological factors influence our behavior, so regardless of whether we can detect pheromones, we just aren't as predictable as pigs.

Despite all of this, however, we can't discard the possibility that we may be constantly transmitting chemical cues to other people, and especially when we're up close and personal, attached at the lips. But that doesn't mean we should fall for all those perfume and cologne companies bombarding us with advertisements and claiming to include human pheromones in their scents. It sure sounds enticing, but the bottom line is that science has yet to unravel the mystery of human pheromone exchange. Without more definitive research, women are probably better off spending their money on lipstick, while men might benefit most by keeping breath mints on hand.

THE TENOR OF THIS discussion raises an interesting question: Have the customs of modern society caused us to shroud our most attractive asset—our scent—under a blanket of soap, perfumes, and other commercially created products? And would we behave differently without so many of these products and the artificial aromas they create? Maybe that's why long-term human relationships are so important—a more natural scent inevitably pokes through as we spend extended periods of time with someone, and may cue us in to the value of the match. Further, what's unpleasant to one person probably tantalizes another.

In any case, I expect we will hear a great deal more about pheromones, and about genetic compatibility in relationships, in the coming years. In fact, a Boston-based Internet dating website called ScientificMatch.com already offers to find you a date based not only on attractiveness or your personal values, but also on your genetic composition.

ScientificMatch.com uses DNA from a cheek swab and runs a "genetic matching algorithm" to locate a partner. According to the website, a lifetime membership costs $1,995.95, but ScientificMatch promises that with a good DNA-based pair-up, customers can achieve a more satisfying sex life, a higher rate of orgasm in women, less cheating, higher fertility, and healthier children. Or as their online banner reads, "Thinking of bringing the relationship to the 'next level'? Not sure if they're really 'the one'? Consider another piece of the puzzle—check your DNA."

This may be the way things are going, but it sounds like our noses have evolved to do a pretty good job without going through all the trouble.

What His Nose Knows

In 2000, psychologists in Texas conducted a study similar to Wedekind's experiment. Seventeen women—who, importantly, were not using hormonal contraceptives at the time—wore the same T-shirt to bed for three consecutive nights, first during the fertile ovulatory phase of their menstrual cycle and then again during their non-ovulatory period. Afterward, the shirts were collected and frozen.

When the shirts were thawed, fifty-two male participants volunteered to rate their scents based on intensity and pleasantness. And sure enough, the shirts worn during the women's ovulatory phase were consistently rated as more attractive and sexy.

Furthermore, when the same shirts were retested a week later after sitting at room temperature, the results were similar. This suggests that the relevant odors do not dissipate immediately, so it's possible men may be employing their noses more than they realize when choosing a partner. In turn, their preferences may be influenced by female fertility, and kissing provides the time and proximity for an adequate sample of a woman's scent.

CHAPTER 8

Close Encounters

Remember that scene in *Pretty Woman* when prostitute Vivian Ward (played by Julia Roberts) explains she'll have sex with—but not kiss—her clients? Apparently the writers for the film did their research: Refraining from mouth-to-mouth kissing has been common among women of the "oldest profession" for a very long time. Social scientists Joanna Brewis and Stephen Linstead report that prostitutes often won't kiss because it requires a "genuine desire and love for the other person." By avoiding the lips of a client, they are best able to keep emotions out of their work.

What about the preferences of those on the flip side of the experience—the so-called johns? Sex therapist Martha Stein watched as sixty-four prostitutes had sex with their clients for a total of 1,230 encounters. Using hidden one-way mirrors and tape recorders, she ensured the men could not detect her presence. Stein reported that just 36 percent of johns wanted to kiss the prostitute somewhere on her body, and only 13 percent were interested in French kissing.

These examples demonstrate that kissing seems fully removable, in certain contexts, from sex for sheer pleasure. Both prostitutes and their clients instinctively seem to sense there is more to a kiss than to other sexual acts—that it's in a different category. And indeed, in social surveys, people rate kissing as more intimate than almost every other kind of activity. It also garners more attention in serious relationships than in casual sexual encounters, and scientists are discovering some fascinating reasons why. The warm fuzzy feelings that we attach to kissing probably have a lot to do with the hormones coursing through our bodies as a result.

As we've already learned, kissing someone you care about and crave releases multiple neurotransmitters and endorphins that serve to relieve stress, regulate mood, and lower blood pressure. It's a natural upper with the power to stimulate feelings of euphoria. But there's much more going on than that. Hormones are involved too, and while they share many similarities with neurotransmitters, there is an important difference in how and where they are released in the body, and the kinds of effects they can generate.

Humans produce a long list of hormones, from estrogen and testosterone to insulin and cortisol, which modulate bodily activities relating to growth, development, reproduction, and metabolism. Glands in our endocrine system—including the thyroid, parathyroid, adrenal, pituitary, pancreas, hypothalamus, and most of all the ovaries and testes—produce different hormones and release them into the bloodstream. From there, these molecules circulate in order to act on a target somewhere else in the body. In this way, hormones differ from neurotransmitters, which are sent directly from a nerve cell to a destination in a much quicker (and less sustained) transfer.

It helps to imagine these two different kinds of chemical agents as being akin to two people communicating by letters. A hormone would put a postage stamp on hers and send it out in the mail. It may be slow, but she's confident her recipient will eventually read what she wrote. The neurotransmitter, though, is on edge. He has his target's personal address and walks directly to its door, shoving his message in the mail slot. A neurotransmitter's delivery is quick and direct, happening in milliseconds. Hormones, on the other hand, can take seconds or even months to have an effect, and that effect lasts much longer. (Complicating matters further, some substances, like oxytocin, can function as both hormone and neurotransmitter, depending on where they're working in the body.)

Hormones influence our behaviors and our emotions. They regulate a woman's body throughout her reproductive years, causing the uncomfortable changes associated with premenstrual syndrome (PMS). Later in life, they are also the reason for hot flashes during menopause.

Less obviously, hormones can even affect the way we taste to a partner. At the onset of menstruation, a woman's body sheds special cells in the lining of her mouth, and this can cause the growth of excess bacteria. Similarly, estrogen can lead to higher than normal oral sulfur concentrations. Both situations can cause her to have bad breath.

Hormones are not exactly easy on men, either. Testosterone can lead to all sorts of embarrassing situations right around the time puberty hits. It deepens men's voices and causes excess hair growth in some places—and eventually contributes to the loss of it on top of their heads. Hormones can also drive some men to act like aggressive brutes or even sexual predators. In short, they plague both sexes with inconvenient upheavals throughout our lives.

But aside from the trials and tribulations associated with hormonal vicissitudes, they also maintain our general health and well-being. So while they can be annoying and uncomfortable, hormones are also crucial and involved in many vital activities, ranging from breast milk production to mood regulation. They literally drive our behaviors and are also responsible for nudging us to propagate the human species.

Humans aren't slaves to these motivational substances, but an intricate dance takes place between our chemistry and our consciousness. Hormones and neurotransmitters do not "create" our emotions; they merely instruct our brains to produce a series of responses, which in turn motivate us to do things like create art, cook dinner, and even experience the romance of a special kiss. They're always at work sending out subconscious signals that tell us how to behave and feel in the world we inhabit. So do not think of them as independent molecules. Rather, they're a fundamental part of who we are.

KISSING ANOTHER PERSON GREATLY shapes the ebb and flow of hormones through our bodies. The pattern of responses is laid down early; the hormones released in the body of a nursing baby girl, for instance, influence the responses she will have later in life. As an adult, she will experience positive emotions when she is kissed, hugged, massaged, and touched—thanks to the very same hormones once associated with nursing in infancy.

Hormones may also explain some of the gender divisions around kissing that show up repeatedly, some of which we've already encountered—but there are many other similar examples. Social surveys report that men overwhelmingly prefer wet, sloppy, openmouthed kisses. Women, on the other hand, are more likely to opt for less saliva and tongue. There's every reason to think these tendencies have a great deal to do with the principal male sex hormone, testosterone.

Men naturally produce greater quantities of testosterone than women, but women are more sensitive to its influence. This amazing little molecule raises a woman's libido and engorges her clitoris with blood—priming her for sex—so a little extra dose via a partner's mouth may be very much to his sexual and reproductive advantage. Since a man's saliva contains his testosterone, swirling his tongue into a woman's mouth is a way to legally slip her a natural sex stimulant.

Over weeks and months of kissing, scientists theorize that she may become more interested in getting physical. It's not something that would happen in one night, but as her suitor persists over time, the influence of added testosterone may have a cumulative effect. This provides ample reason for a man to continue pursuing the woman he's been kissing, and also explains why men are more likely to view kissing as a prelude to sex, and to report the preference for more tongue. While women may not enjoy a sloppy kissing experience as much, it can give men an added sexual advantage, and has probably been a successful strategy throughout history.

A second possibility that has been suggested to explain why men prefer deep kissing has to do with the fact that they are less sensitive to smell and taste (technically termed "reduced chemosensory detection"). This could mean that a man requires a much larger saliva sample during a kiss than a woman does in order to assess a partner. Added tongue movement would provide increased exposure to her saliva, and additional time for him to obtain hidden clues about her reproductive status. However, scientists aren't sure how much can be subconsciously inferred about female fertility through this kind of exchange, so while the hypothesis is interesting, it's also speculative.

. . .

AND INCIDENTALLY, WHEN IT comes to male preferences for tongue-kissing, I couldn't pass up another opportunity to query my friends to see if survey trends held. When I asked around, they most definitely did. Men frequently added that lots of oral action provided insight into how a particular partner might perform sexually. Conversely, most women complained that "too much tongue" is a turnoff. Once again, my acquaintances do not constitute a scientifically valid sample, but their stated tastes emphasize the way that men's and women's kissing preferences have been influenced by strategies that have evolved over millions of years.

Of course, many hormones beyond testosterone are involved in kissing. And when it comes to pinning down their role—not always an easy task—neuroscientists Wendy Hill and Carey Wilson of Lafayette College have been conducting some fascinating research. Their methodology involves inviting college-aged couples to kiss in a controlled setting, while their team carefully collects information about the changes going on in the volunteers' bodies. They are most interested in the role of two main hormonal players: oxytocin and cortisol. So before we get into discussing their research, let's meet these molecules in more detail.

Often called the "love hormone," oxytocin is inextricably involved in intimacy, and has been shown to have extremely powerful effects in a laboratory setting. For example, when it is injected into the brain of a virgin female rat, this hormone causes her to immediately adopt the babies of another rat as her own. Nobody has tried the above experiment in women (for reasons that are perhaps obvious), but we know oxytocin works similarly in our own species. It is responsible for cementing the connection between parent and child and also serves to trigger lactation in new mothers. It helps to regulate mood and acts as a natural painkiller.

But here's the most interesting aspect for our purposes: Oxytocin is very important in developing feelings of attachment, not just to our mothers but to our lovers. Scientists believe it is the substance that keeps love alive in couples that stay together happily over decades, long after the novelty (and the dopamine) has worn off. Thanks to oxytocin, a kiss, a hug, or a warm caress can help maintain a solid and strong attachment. And it's important to take the physical affection further, too. When a woman has sex, levels of oxytocin can peak up to five times higher than normal, and it is the substance responsible for the pleasurable "jolts" she feels in her pelvis during orgasm. Studies in men have also revealed that the hormone can spike three to five times higher than normal during sexual climax. Oxytocin is a force of nature.

Furthermore, this hormone may explain why the suggestion to "kiss and make up" works so well. When asked why they kiss, men often report that it helps to resolve a disagreement. Although most women surveyed claim a kiss doesn't make things better automatically, evolutionary psychologists disagree: It can. Research has demonstrated that a kiss or series of kisses tend to foster a woman's forgiveness. It sounds formulaic, but when it comes to the rules of engagement, hormones don't play fair.

Cortisol, meanwhile, is known as the "stress hormone," and has a central role in our body's responses to anxiety or threat. When released, it raises blood pressure and blood sugar, while suppressing our immune response. Cortisol is the reason we can be amped to do well on a test or in a public presentation, and then crash afterward. Too much of the hormone can be a bad thing, but in more moderate amounts it helps to restore stability in our bodies after stressful periods. In healthy people, cortisol levels rise and fall on a daily cycle.

Hill and Wilson are interested in learning more about how concentrations of oxytocin and cortisol in the body change before and after kissing a partner—and how this, in turn, may promote bonding between lovers. At the outset of their research, the scientists hypothesized that kissing would enhance bonding through hormonal changes, and expected to find that it leads to increased levels of oxytocin and decreased levels of cortisol.

To that end, their team at Lafayette College recruited fifteen heterosexual couples aged eighteen to twenty-two who were in long-term relationships (averaging 560 days). The experiment took place at possibly the least romantic setting on campus, the university's student health center. At the outset, each study subject had blood drawn and spit in a cup to provide what's called "baseline information" (the body's levels before the experiment) on both hormones. Next, the couples were organized into two groups. Half were instructed to kiss their partner with mouths open, while the rest were told to hold hands and talk. In my favorite anecdote from the experiment, one relieved female participant assigned to kiss her boyfriend remarked to Hill, "Thank God, because I didn't have anything to talk to him about if we were put in the other group!"

The experimental group followed their kissing orders, and the couples in the control group carried on a conversation with each other for sixteen minutes. Afterward, everyone provided another saliva and blood sample and filled out questionnaires about their personality, current levels of stress, and the degree of intimacy in their relationship. The women were also asked about their menstrual cycles and whether they used birth control, since these details might impact the results (for instance, women on birth control had higher baseline levels of oxytocin than those not taking the pill).

Hill and Wilson found that the stress hormone, cortisol, decreased across both groups, regardless of whether couples were kissing or holding hands. Thus it appears that affectionate behavior has real health benefits; it cuts stress. What's more, when we're relaxed, we're also more likely to want to take things to the next physical level.

Curiously though, oxytocin did not behave at all as expected. It appeared to decrease in women, while rising in men. The length of a couple's relationship did not affect the strength of response. The scientists had anticipated that they would see an increase in oxytocin across sexes, and were very puzzled by this result. But then, if experiments always went according to plan, it wouldn't be science.

So what might have been going on? In research, we must always look for factors outside of a study's explicit design that could bias the results. In this particular kissing study, there may have been one large inherent flaw: location. The scientists theorized that women might require more than just kissing to feel sexually excited or connected to a partner; they may need other mood-inducing elements. The sterile, unromantic health facility environment could explain why they experienced the opposite response from what was expected.

The Lafayette team decided to repeat their study, paying more attention to the ambiance. They set the scene, providing jazz music, flowers, and even electric candles for an added touch. They moved a couch into a secluded room in the back of an academic building on campus, rather than conducting trials at the health facility.

The second experiment included nine heterosexual couples and three lesbian couples. This time, the researchers also considered a third hormone called alpha-amylase, which provides another measure of stress and is related to our sympathetic nervous system. The average relationship length for the participants during these trials was 564 days. As before, the couples were divided into two groups. The "control" couples spoke, but did not touch each other, during their encounter, while the experimental pairs kissed for a set duration of time.

The outcome was even more perplexing this time. Once again, cortisol levels decreased for everyone, but both women and men had lower levels of oxytocin at the end of the experiment than at the beginning—precisely the opposite of what was expected. Levels of alpha-amylase did not change. Interestingly, the heterosexual women reported feeling a greater increase in intimacy with their partners than either the men or homosexual women did, but the extremely small sample size makes it impossible to draw any conclusions about the reasons for this.

Overall, these results pose intriguing questions about the way kissing influences our bodies, especially since neither study reflected the trends anticipated. The team has not yet conducted any follow-up research, but they are interested in returning to the topic with a larger sample size in the future. For now, they are working to improve their means of analyzing oxytocin through saliva samples, and are considering running follow-up studies in college residence halls. That way, kissing might take place in a more natural and comfortable setting, and couples would only need to provide a spit sample afterward. (These factors might limit anxiety.)

This experiment represents a classic example of how science isn't always predictable, and sometimes surprises the researchers involved. It also demonstrates how difficult it is to study such an emotional subject as kissing. We know oxytocin increases from feelings of closeness, and that kissing promotes bonding between lovers, so it's a true puzzle why these studies didn't turn out differently. When the experimental procedure improves, I suspect scientists will observe that oxytocin rises in men and women from kissing—just as we already know it does during sex.

Nearly every scientific study raises new questions, and Hill and Wilson's is no exception. For example, how much does the kissing environment really matter in terms of our hormonal response? Would similar trends appear in couples who have been together for much longer or shorter periods of time? If future analyses determine that oxytocin rises from kissing a partner as expected, could kissing soothe a troubled relationship? Quite possibly it could.

But there's a darker side, too, to all that saliva exchange. Not every kiss benefits its practitioners, and kissing isn't always healthy, or even sanitary. In the next chapter, we'll explore the thing we all feared most in grade school: *cooties*.

The Effects of Testosterone
on Women

*W*hen women are exposed to artificially high levels of testosterone through steroid use or gender reassignment, they develop more body hair and a deeper voice, and may feel more aggressive. The clitoris can extend a couple of centimeters as well.

The average heterosexual woman needn't be concerned, though. The amount of testosterone transmitted in a kiss is many orders of magnitude smaller.

CHAPTER 9

There Are Such Things as Cooties

An intensive care unit nurse I know sees all sorts of strange and disturbing illnesses. When I told her that I was writing this book, she quipped, "Maybe the germs are the ones making *us* do the kissing." Swapping spit is such an ideal way of spreading germs that it may be more in their interest than in ours.

While I wouldn't necessarily go that far, it's certainly true that there are many possible illnesses associated with kissing. The human mouth is a filthy place and serves as the breeding ground for legions of bacteria—the microscopic one-celled organisms that keep the antibacterial soap industry booming. Evolutionary biologists Atomz and Avishag Zahavi even suggest that merely accepting a kiss might indicate a partner's high level of commitment. After all, it means he or she is willing to risk acquiring someone else's illness in order to embrace and connect.

This chapter considers the utterly unromantic side of kissing, centered on hygiene and disease. In these days of pandemic fears and H1N1 flu, it's a very necessary part of the story. The goal isn't to frighten you: Generally speaking, readers have little to fear, health-wise, from a kiss. Between most individuals, even the French variety is highly unlikely to prove dangerous. But it's valuable to know just what we're exposing ourselves to when we decide that someone's worth the germs—as many of our loved ones certainly are.

THE AVERAGE BACTERIA'S LIFE is pretty dull. It consumes nutrients from its environment and grows to twice its size; then it divides into two. No big party, simply an exceedingly successful strategy practiced by the oldest living organisms on earth.

We host an overwhelming number of these foreign bacterial cells inside of us, without which we could not hope to survive. Our bodies are made up of about a trillion human cells, but at any moment we also have about ten trillion bacterial cells in or on us. When you add up all of the DNA living in a person, it turns out that we contain around thirty thousand human genes and three million bacterial genes. As Princeton University molecular biologist Bonnie Bassler points out, this means we're arguably just 1 percent human and 99 percent bacteria! Most of these bacteria help us by absorbing nutrients, digesting food, producing vitamins, and supporting our immune system, but when the "bad" bacteria take up residence, we can become sick.

Kissing is a very effective way to share these little guys. Our saliva has many important functions—it allows us to taste food (and our kissing partner) by lubricating our taste buds with a protein called mucin—but it is also an ideal conduit for bacteria, of both the good and bad variety. During the 1950s, Baltimore City College's Dr. Owen Hendley determined that 278 colonies of bacteria could be passed between kissers, although over 95 percent were of the harmless sort. Nevertheless, the numbers game is pretty stunning when you consider that our saliva contains about one hundred million bacteria per milliliter. For reference, one milliliter of saliva is about the size of a die on a Las Vegas craps table.

One of the first risks from these bugs is dental decay, the most common human malady around the world. A particularly nasty strain in this respect is *Lactobacillus acidophilus*, which feasts on chewed but unswallowed starch and sugar (the morsels stuck between our teeth after a meal). Through the process of fermentation, the bacteria transforms them into a substance called lactic acid, which in turn eats away at our enamel and encourages more bacterial reproduction, perpetuating the cycle of tooth decay.

Susceptibility to cavities is highly varied among individuals, meaning that some of us are far more affected than others. So if your partner's mouth harbors an above-average bacteria count, you may actually run the risk of getting additional cavities yourself as a result. That doesn't mean you should shy away from an otherwise healthy relationship based on the number of fillings you spot. Regular brushing and flossing should keep your own bacterial concentration under control regardless.

Tooth decay is just one of the risks posed by bacteria that travel through our mouths. While we're still on the subject of oral hygiene, let's consider something a bit more disturbing, though fortunately mostly benign: a so-called fuzzy tongue.

You may occasionally notice a thin, colored film carpeting your partner's tongue. The soft grassy layer may look disconcerting (especially if it's yellow or brown). This condition can occur when heavy doses of antibiotics kill off the beneficial bacteria in our mouths, allowing a nastier variety to take up residence. Should you ever encounter this phenomenon, the bearer of fuzz probably deserves the benefit of the doubt—so wait a few days before making any judgment about his or her hygiene habits. Still, it's advisable to avoid mouth-to-mouth contact until things clear up. You wouldn't want to contract any kind of lingering illness that required the antibiotics to begin with.

And there are still other, lesser-known types of bacteria that can exploit the human kiss. In 1982, Drs. Barry

Marshall and Robin Warren discovered that a bacterium called *Helicobacter pylori* is commonly responsible for causing ulcers. This bug weakens the protective coating of the stomach and the upper part of the small intestine, allowing stomach acid to get through. Thus while ulcers have multiple causes—they can result from stress or spicy food, among other things—we now know one prominent trigger is a microscopic organism lurking in our mouths. Scientists are still not entirely sure how *H. pylori* moves between people, but it has been found in saliva, leading many doctors to speculate that kissing may be one cause. (Fortunately, even though nearly one out of five people under the age of forty carries *H. pylori*, most do not develop ulcers.)

Moving beyond these relatively harmless conditions, there's also a troubling correlation between a teenager's number of kissing partners and the likelihood that he or she will develop dangerous bacterial meningitis. This frightening disease causes inflammation of the meninges (membranes covering the brain and spinal cord) and a condition known as septicemia (blood poisoning). Meningitis symptoms include a high fever, vomiting, severe headache, joint and muscle pains, stomach cramps, diarrhea, cold hands and feet, and sensitivity to light. The condition can be fatal.

A 2006 study published in the *British Medical Journal* examined 144 teenagers aged fifteen to nineteen who had been diagnosed with meningitis. The researchers found that openmouthed kissing of multiple partners was associated with a heightened risk of illness. Still, bear in mind that there are many correlated factors *not linked* directly with kissing that also increase the chance of contracting meningitis. Furthermore, I suspect that the statistics cited above are heavily influenced by the lifestyles of the demographic being studied, which poses a higher risk than average. For example, a crowded dormitory with shared bathrooms probably provides more opportunities than average for exposure to disease.

Perhaps the most worrisome thing about bacteria is not the conditions they currently cause, but those they might cause in the future. In our germophobic society, bacteria are known to be growing stronger. Through an onslaught of antibacterial hand soaps, cleansers, and unnecessary prescription antibiotics, humans have unwittingly bred resistant strains of bacteria that survive and reproduce when their weaker compatriots perish. We have created superbugs that are increasingly immune to medical treatments, and deadlier than ever before.

Today many microbiologists fear another pandemic like the Black Death will occur once we can no longer cure the bacterial infections that have evolved a resistance to our best drugs. Staphylococcus and streptococcus ("staph" and "strep" infections) are two bacterial strains that are becoming increasingly resistant to antibiotics, and ever more worrisome to health care professionals. Streptococcal bacteria caused the untimely death of Muppets creator Jim Henson at the age of fifty-three. A growing number of people are walking around carrying colonies of dangerous antibiotic-resistant strains like methicillin-resistant staphylococcus aureus (MRSA), oxacillin-resistant staph aureus (ORSA), and vancomycin-resistant enterococcus (VRE). Should these enter the bloodstream through breaks in the skin (including in the mouth) they can become very dangerous.

BUT BACTERIA are only one type of germ that can be transmitted through a kiss. Viruses also enter our bodies, where they grow, reproduce, and spread to make us sick. About a hundred times smaller than bacteria, they too can cause all sorts of mayhem. Many are capable of invading and ultimately killing off individual cells. Some viruses reproduce without causing a malignancy, but other strains have been proven to cause diseases like cervical cancer, smallpox, human immunodeficiency virus (HIV), and polio.

The odds are good that at least one viral kissing-related danger will be intimately familiar to you. Many people reading this book right now already carry this virus in their bodies, and once you do, you become a host for life. I'm referring to herpes simplex 1 (HSV-1), which is easily transmitted and causes reddish or purple cold sores on the outer edge of the lip. Sometimes these blisters occur in bunches, and they can be filled with fluid before scabbing over and disappearing. They may be unsightly and embarrassing, but are not otherwise dangerous except in very rare cases. (Another strain called HSV-2 can cause oral sores as well, but is more commonly associated with genital herpes, and also lasts for life.)

While HSV-1 is commonly associated with romantic kissing, it can also be obtained by the sharing of eating utensils, toothbrushes, or even by social kisses between friends and relatives. Once we're infected, you might say the virus unpacks and gets comfortable. While many people who are carriers never show the symptoms of HSV-1, lesions can burn before breakout and emerge painfully. An eruption can be triggered by getting a cold, excessive exposure to the sun, stress, a lip injury, or even dental work.

In truth, it's nearly impossible to avoid this virus as we go about our lives: An estimated 50 percent of us have acquired HSV-1 by the time we reach our teens, and 80 to 90 percent of the population tests positive by age fifty. With figures like that, there shouldn't be any stigma associated with HSV-1, but the statistics were of no consolation to a good friend of mine in high school. Her cold sores forced her to suffer through years of taunting by boys who very likely also carried the same virus. I advised her not to pay them any mind because, after all, the real "freaks" are those of us who do not wind up as hosts.

Of course, it's the Epstein-Barr virus (EBV), another type of herpes virus, that's responsible for the "kissing disease," better known as mononucleosis, or "mono." It's also very common. Up to 95 percent of American adults have been infected, and carry and spread the virus, on and off, throughout their lives.

In childhood, EBV symptoms are generally indistinguishable from those of other illnesses, and may disappear quickly. But during adolescence, EBV causes infectious mononucleosis, accompanied by a fever 35 to 50 percent of the time. The condition brings about inflated lymph glands, a sore throat, and sometimes a swollen liver or spleen. It can make a person feel achy all over and tired. Occasionally there are more serious problems, but the virus is rarely fatal. While it's carried in saliva and can be spread through kissing, you can get it in all sorts of other ways—by sharing straws, pillows, food, spoons, and forks.

One virus you probably do not need to be concerned about when it comes to kissing is HIV. Although many people suffer from bleeding gums, the virus does not appear to be transmitted this way. It's probably safe to kiss your partner passionately without first sending him or her to a clinic for analysis.

To date, no one on record has become infected with HIV from kisses without tongue. Openmouthed kissing, meanwhile, is considered a low-risk activity by the Centers for Disease Control and Prevention (CDC), and there's only one case where a woman apparently contracted HIV through her kissing partner's contaminated blood. (The details in this case are unclear, and curiously, the man involved was reported as a "sexual partner" as well.) Still, the CDC warns against "prolonged open-mouth kissing" with someone known to carry HIV.

Something else you needn't worry about is locking braces: This appears to be an urban legend. Modern braces are smaller than they were in the past, and according to the American Association of Orthodontists, it is nearly impossible to get stuck to someone while kissing—braces, after all, are not magnetic.

AND THEN there are the riskiest "kisses" of all. Fortunately, they are probably unfamiliar to most readers, since they involve going to extraordinarily dangerous extremes. Still, it's important to survey the most unusual styles of "kissing" behavior that can lead to dire consequences.

The recent rise of interest in vampires, particularly among teens, makes the practice of biting another person to draw their blood necessary to mention. In short, just don't do it. Swapping saliva through traditional kissing is vastly safer than literally injecting gobs of potentially dangerous microorganisms directly into the bloodstream of your beloved. It's probably the worst conceivable way to show someone you care, given that you're exposing them to a potentially life-threatening situation.

Many of the germs in our mouths are harmless until they break the skin barrier. In fact, doctors consider the human bite to be of greater concern than most snakebites and broken bones, and often send human bite victims straight to the emergency room. So remember the lesson from preschool and do not bite your loved ones for any reason. The outcome won't be as sensual as it appears on film, and may require medical intervention.

Along the same lines, it's also inadvisable to make any kind of oral contact with the mouths of wild animals that could be carrying deadly diseases. In the summer of 2009, for instance, the Lee County Health Department in Florida and the CDC put out a search for three boys, aged ten to twelve years old, who had been seen "kissing" a dead rabid bat in Florida. Who knows what they were thinking, but they took a tremendous risk. There is no cure for rabies.

Fortunately, the average person will not encounter these uniquely dangerous kinds of "kisses." But there is one further risk that can truly put you in a life-or-death situation.

You might think you're out with the perfect person, about to embark on an epic romance. All the signals seem right, and you go in for the kiss. But suddenly, instead of being excited and aroused, you—or your partner—is covered with hives. Oscar Wilde once remarked, "A kiss may ruin a human life." While I doubt he had peanut butter or split pea soup in mind, allergens can be a serious mood killer, or in extreme cases even a deadly poison.

For the majority of us, this scenario has probably never crossed our minds. But food sensitivities can rear their ugly heads at the most inopportune time. The usual suspects are shellfish, eggs, and milk, but peanut allergies are the main cause of fatalities. In extreme cases, kissing has triggered an immediate anaphylactic reaction from contact with trace amounts of the substance on another person's lips. Symptoms can develop quickly and without warning—including difficulty breathing, facial swelling, hives, a dangerous drop in blood pressure, shock, loss of consciousness, and sometimes death.

A recent study published in the *New England Journal of Medicine* found that about 5 percent of people who are allergic to nuts or seeds reported experiencing adverse reactions from kissing. When seventeen volunteers consented to be kissed by someone who had just consumed their particular allergen, reactions occurred in under a minute, and involved itching and swelling. Some subjects experienced wheezing, and one required a shot of epinephrine in the emergency room. These results suggest that although kissing isn't normally considered a life-threatening activity, food allergies do threaten a small percentage of the population—even after a partner has brushed his or her teeth.

IF YOU'RE FEELING SQUEAMISH about puckering up at this point, you're not alone. There's an actual term, "philematophobia": the fear of kissing, which occurs when someone comes to find lip-on-lip contact completely terrifying. Some people who suffer from this are most frightened of bacteria, while others fear having their tongues bitten off.

Most of us, though, want to keep kissing—while protecting ourselves from potential disease. By any measure, an awareness of the risks described above is a key part of our defenses. Not only can cleanliness help defeat germs, but it also boosts the likelihood that another virus- and bacteria-laden mouth pressed to yours will be back for more.

No matter how attractive someone may be, poor hygiene can kill the moment before it even begins. This is particularly true for men. As preceding chapters have described, women depend heavily on taste and smell and pay close attention to teeth when evaluating a partner.

In this chapter, I've covered the disturbing, dirty, and allergic aspects of kissing. In the end, it certainly seems the practice can leave us exposed to some serious illnesses. Still, claims about "risk" mean nothing without context, and when it comes to kissing, the risks are relatively minor compared to other sexual and nonsexual activities. In reality, there are generally a greater number of dangerous germs transmitted during a handshake than a kiss.

Furthermore, some noteworthy benefits to kissing should be balanced against concerns. For example, thinking about a desirable kiss stimulates the flow of your own saliva, bathing the mouth and dispersing plaque, which helps protect your teeth.

And aside from improving our mood, being on a natural kissing high may also help us live longer. A ten-year psychology study undertaken in Germany during the 1980s found that men who kissed their wives before leaving for work lived, on average, five years longer, earning 20 to 30 percent more than peers who left without a peck good-bye. The researchers also reported that *not* kissing one's wife before leaving in the morning increased the possibility of a car accident by 50 percent. Psychologists do not believe it's the kiss itself that accounts for the difference but rather that kissers were likely to begin the day with a positive attitude, leading to a healthier lifestyle. Kissing, after all, has been proven to promote strong social bonds, which have been shown to foster health benefits and emotional well-being.

So although kissing carries some risk, it also brings potential rewards. And no matter what the medical experts may discover, I have a feeling humans will keep at it for a very long time.

The Blarney Stone

*I*n 2009, the travel website TripAdvisor.com dubbed the Blarney Stone in Cork, Ireland, the most "unhygienic" tourist attraction in the world.

Why so disgusting? Every day, over a thousand visitors kiss the stone at Blarney Castle, which is purported to give people the gift of eloquent speech. To reach it, they must literally bend over backward and hang on to iron bars. Despite the trouble, up to 400,000 people press their lips to its surface each year. No doubt that's a lot of germs, but TripAdvisor.com admits it has no scientific evidence to back the claim that it's truly the germiest destination on earth. 🖎

PART THREE

Great
Expectations

Kisses are a better fate than wisdom.

—e. e. cummings

CHAPTER 10

This Is Your Brain
on Kissing

O ne evening while I was researching this book, I found myself staring down a mountain of scientific articles related to kissing. And suddenly it occurred to me: Given how much I'd already learned about the subject, there must be a way to push existing knowledge a little bit further and make some new discoveries. After conducting a thorough search of the scientific literature on kissing, I knew very well what kind of research was already out there—including many of the studies discussed in the preceding pages. It wasn't all that much compared to what exists in other scientific fields; you would think a near-universal behavior in our species might have garnered more attention. Still, there was no doubt that the science to date raised a lot of interesting—and testable—possibilities.

For instance, if men and women have different hormonal responses to kissing (as shown in chapter 8), these changes would be intimately related to what's going on in our brains during the behavior. After all, the brain controls the release of our hormones. So how would the response to a kiss appear when recorded using the latest brain imaging technology? Might we visualize differences between the sexes?

As far as I could tell from my research, no one had yet studied kissing using a brain scanning device like a magnetoencephalography (MEG) machine, capable of picking up a far different kind of information than revealed by surveys or blood and saliva tests. Wondering how I might obtain access to such a machine, I called up a friend in neuroscience, Dr. David Poeppel, to find out if I could tear him away from his research at New York University long enough to begin a new investigation on kissing and the brain.

And here's the crazy part: He agreed.

Poeppel is a cognitive neuroscientist who's interested in the way our brains are involved in human hearing and speech, and how they store and perceive information. He's also exploring the brain-to-computer interface: Might our thoughts be downloadable and transferable and even emailable, just like other bits of data? Just when you thought reading minds was pure science fiction, David is out to write the true story. (Don't worry, though. Even if it is possible, he assures me that mind control would not be feasible for an extremely long time.)

Poeppel has the kind of intense curiosity that makes for

a great scientist, and on top of that he's also very cool. He's not the stereotypical scientist depicted by Hollywood as a socially awkward Rick Moranis character or an evildoer out to take over the world. Instead, David's a funny, really nice family man with a great team of graduate students. He also happens to have access to several amazing and powerful brain scanning machines in his NYU laboratory.

I'm not sure David knew what he was getting into when I initially contacted him, but he seemed keen to hear my ideas for the next steps in kissing experimentation. After a two-hour conversation, I bought tickets to fly several hundred miles up to his lab in New York City. We began laying out the methodology for a scientific study that, to the best of our knowledge, had never before been attempted—a cognitive neuroscience experiment on the effect of kissing in the brain.

MAGNETOENCEPHALOGRAPHY provides a unique way of looking at how our brains work. Scientists call it a "brain imaging" technique, but what an MEG machine really does is measure the magnetic fields produced by the everyday electrical impulses in our brains. It allows scientists to watch brain activity as it happens, and study the direction and location of the impulses that are the basis for all our thoughts and actions, ranging from instinctive muscle movements to the release of various neurotransmitters.

What's more, MEG is noninvasive, meaning that we can see these magnetic fields—which reflect ongoing brain activity—without any surgery or risk to the research subject.

An MEG machine is also a rare, expensive piece of hardware that runs several millions of dollars. There are only about ten or fifteen of them in the entire United States. But despite the cost, the machine is rather underwhelming in person. When you go inside its small magnetically shielded room to have your brain scanned, the table you have to lie down on doesn't look much different from the standard examination table at the doctor's office. Meanwhile, the place where you stick your head so that all this high-tech science can happen sort of resembles a toilet bowl. The walls of Poeppel's MEG are constructed out of a special material called Mμ—an expensive mixture of metals with a high level of magnetic permeability. Mμ creates an environment that's uniquely silent because it's magnetically shielded from the outside world.

If we were going to study kissing with this sophisticated and yet humble contraption, we would first have to get around an obvious practical problem: Two people can't simultaneously squeeze their heads inside the machine's "toilet" to make out. And even if they could, reading brain scans while subjects kissed would be nearly impossible, because they wouldn't be holding still. Moreover, the context of the situation would be way too weird to extract any useful information. Cramped quarters, strange electrodes, and overlapping wires would undoubtedly skew the kissing experience. Just think of what a too-clinical hospital environment probably did to Hill and Wilson's study of kissing and hormones, and multiply the effect dramatically.

But in conversations with David, we soon thought of a way around this problem. One thing we *could* do with the MEG was show individual test subjects images of different couples kissing so as to evoke an observable brain response, and then measure it. In fact, this would introduce a new novelty into the experiment. As far as David knew, few MEG studies had looked at subjects' responses to viewing *two* individuals doing something together (like kissing). Generally, human images used in past MEG studies had been simpler, such as displaying a single face.

Now we had a good strategy—but the approach quickly raised another problem. Since science has no official taxonomy of kisses—i.e., no standard way to categorize all the different kinds—I would first need to establish one before we could show any kissing images to test subjects. Different kinds of kisses would surely evoke different brain responses; but we couldn't measure them until we had decided precisely what kinds of kisses we wished to show.

So after a good deal of thinking, and after remembering some kissing taxonomies from the Kama Sutra and from

Roman times, I finally settled on three kissing "categories" to include:

1. EROTIC KISS: passionate/sexually charged kiss
2. FRIENDSHIP KISS: kiss between friends
3. RELATIONSHIP KISS: affectionate kiss implying commitment

As we've seen, there are many other types of kisses in the world. But collecting a range of images fitting these precise categories—and ensuring, at the same time, that the people in the images did not show major differences in age, race, or other attributes that might skew a subject's responses—was more than enough work for a preliminary scientific run.

For this early experiment, we also decided—in a fateful choice for what our results would ultimately show, though I didn't know it then—that our three types of kisses would further vary according to three "conditions." In addition to being either "erotic," "friendship," or "relationship" kisses, the kissing pairings in the images would be either male-female, female-female, or male-male. In the end, this meant that we would be scanning our test subjects' brains to see how they responded to a total of nine different kinds of kisses, as follows:

The Nine "Conditions" of the Kissing-MEG Experiment

EROTIC Male-Female	RELATIONSHIP Male-Female	FRIENDSHIP Male-Female
EROTIC Female-Female	RELATIONSHIP Female-Female	FRIENDSHIP Female-Female
EROTIC Male-Male	RELATIONSHIP Male-Male	FRIENDSHIP Male-Male

Finding photos to include in the study was not nearly as easy as it sounds. I began in the obvious way, by scouring the Internet for available images. Not surprisingly, a Google search for terms like "two women kissing" and "erotic kiss" led to all sorts of hits that weren't particularly useful for my intended goal. I also received more than a few strange glances while I worked in North Carolina coffee shops.

After sifting through far more pornography than I'd like to admit, I eventually located fifteen acceptable images whose kissing "category" seemed obvious. I then cropped the photos so they would show only the kissers' heads—that way, their body positions or postures would not influence our test subjects' responses. Furthermore, and to cut out other possible extraneous influences on the test subjects, I converted all the images from color to black-and-white.

While I won't show you here all of the different images used in the study, here is a good example of what one of the "conditions"—female-female relationship—might have looked like:

PHOTO: ARIEL SOTO

Sample image to represent
"female-female committed relationship"

And still, I wasn't nearly finished setting the stage for our study of kissing in an MEG machine. For while I had my own interpretations of what each picture conveyed, and what kissing "category" it belonged to, I wanted to ensure that a suitably large consensus existed among other people as well. After all, perhaps my "erotic" kiss was someone else's "relationship" kiss.

Fortunately, the blog I write for *Discover* magazine attracts a fairly wide audience, so I developed a kissing survey for our readers. On June 8, 2009, I posted all fifteen images online, labeled by the letters A through O, and asked for readers' help. They weren't allowed to comment directly on the blog, because I didn't want them to bias other readers' responses. Rather, everyone interested in replying was asked to email privately with an assessment of each kiss: Was it "erotic," "friendship," or "committed relationship"?

I had hoped for at least fifty responses, a big enough number that I could run some statistics. I'm not sure whom I was kidding. The post got a vast amount of attention and multiple links in from other blogs and websites, and over the following days I received close to a thousand emails about the survey ... and that was only the beginning.

For weeks, they continued pouring in, in vastly greater numbers than I could hope to analyze or process. Some viewers expressed feeling "turned on" by looking at the photos of kissing couples, while a few reported outright disgust. Several suggested ranking each kisser individually, or made recommendations about kissing technique. There were even those who, unsatisfied by the limited options I had provided, went ahead and created new kissing categories separate from my own.

Meanwhile, countless long threads emerged in discussion forums on the Internet, debating the meanings of erotica and commitment based on the images. It seemed everyone had an opinion about them, and while I didn't always agree, I certainly felt very encouraged that so many people were interested.

After spending a day organizing all the survey responses into a spreadsheet, I narrowed the list down to the nine photographs whose interpretation had been most universally agreed upon. At long last, I was ready to take them to New York to show to real live test subjects. The avalanche of responses from the blog survey gave me high hopes for what we might learn in the machine.

ON JULY 5, 2009, I flew to New York to meet with the Poeppel lab. Before we got started, I wanted to learn more about how the MEG machine worked, so I volunteered to be the first guinea pig in a test run.

I changed into a pair of scrubs so no aspect of my clothing would interfere with the machine's magnetic signals. I also had to remove all metallic objects from my body, including jewelry, hairclips, and even my bra. Next, the lab technician, Christine, took digital measurements of my head using a computerized tool shaped like a pencil. I watched as a 3-D image of my head's shape appeared on the screen of a nearby computer. Once we had my skull's precise curvature recorded, Christine taped electrodes across my forehead to monitor its position as I was scanned.

Next, Christine and David led me into the special magnetically shielded room that housed the MEG. By then, with my attire and all the wires on my head, I looked and felt as if I were headed into outer space—but instead, I laid down in the scanner. I asked David about the toilet bowl–like cylinder now surrounding my head, and he explained that liquid helium (a very cold fluid) was circulating through it. I had visions of Mr. Freeze from the *Batman* comics, but it was too late to back out.

Over the intercom, David's assistant, Jeff, instructed me to stay as still as possible, because any movement could change how the magnetic fields from my brain were recorded. At long last, we were ready to begin. Directly above my head I saw a screen where the following message appeared:

Ready...
Thank you for participating in this experiment.
You will now see a series of images of people kissing.
Please pay close attention. Press the far left button if you find the images Erotic, the middle button if the people in the images seem Committed and the far right button for Friendship.
Press any button to begin.

I pushed the button—and watched the nine kissing images I had so carefully selected flash before my eyes in random order, over and over. Each was displayed forty times, for a total of 360 "trials."

Inside the machine, I lost my identity and became test subject 0041—the first of the results we would include in the data set. As I watched the images that I already knew so well flash by, it also dawned on me that the process of writing a book about kissing had now, quite unexpectedly, taken me into a world that I'd never before experienced.

I had been classically trained in the marine sciences; my central scientific experience was in ecology and evolutionary biology. Neuroscience, in practice, was utterly different; and brain imaging was an entirely distinct and new means of understanding human behavior. I felt very much out of my scientific element. But I also felt inspired, and found myself thinking of dozens of questions we could pursue with this new, powerful apparatus. My mind raced with possibilities as kisses flashed before my eyes. I couldn't help wondering whether my busy thoughts would skew the data collection process.

Twenty minutes later I emerged into the computer room, curious as to what all the spikes and squiggles on the monitors—my thoughts, my brain's electrical impulses—really represented. All I had to go on was a "map" of my head, which to me had little more meaning than a hieroglyph.

It was getting near time to bring in the volunteers who would allow us to run them through the same experiment and continue our scientific study. But first David's team asked if I would allow them to put me through another brain scanner as well, their functional magnetic resonance imaging (fMRI) machine. One of the most recently developed devices for brain imaging, an fMRI, unlike an MEG, works by measuring blood activity in the brain or spinal cord. Once again, the machine lets scientists and doctors observe brain behavior without risking radiation exposure or other injury to the subject. How could I say no?

The scientists shoveled me into a tube, which made all sorts of loud banging noises as I stayed as still as possible for thirty minutes. Afterward I got to see my brain onscreen—a pretty surreal experience. I watched as David's assistant Tobias zoomed in and out, passing through my brain as if it were terrain on Google Earth. It dawned on me that all the experiences of my entire life—every birthday and holiday, every public and private moment, including my very first kiss—took place in that intricate mass of tissue and cells. It was the closest I could ever get to observing my soul. Yet onscreen, while Tobias provided the virtual tour, the image appeared clinical. I felt very fortunate for the opportunity to get such an intimate look at myself, but somehow I also felt it wasn't a complete image. Surely there was more to me than the maze of dark and light lines I saw.

At last we returned to the MEG, where our test subjects were now being studied, and I watched the same squiggles dance onscreen for each participant. I wondered why they varied, and which kissing images caused the most intense reactions in each subject (it wasn't possible to tell yet).

David and his team spent three days running subjects

in the machine, as I watched and took notes. Four men and four women in total were scanned, hailing from different parts of the world (China, Israel, Germany, the United States, and Canada). To me, this seemed like a very small sample size; in my own marine biology research I had studied thousands of sea cucumbers. But in human neuroscience, eight is a reasonable number for an early MEG experiment. The small group allows scientists to evaluate whether there is anything to pursue systematically in the future through more extensive study. If they observe a striking or strong result, the research continues.

As the work proceeded, my first question was whether the men and women would respond differently to the different images of kissing. From Gordon Gallup's surveys and Wendy Hill's blood tests, it seems clear that the sexes experience kissing very differently, but what that meant in terms of brain imaging was yet to be determined.

Another question was whether there would be a marked difference when the test subjects viewed homosexual versus heterosexual kissing couples. And then there was the matter of sexual arousal. Men are far more sexually responsive, and far more interested in visually arousing images, than women are. Might the erotic photographs in particular trigger a distinct response in each gender?

I wouldn't be able to get answers to any of these questions right away—rather, I would have to wait until David and his graduate student Gregory could run statistical analyses on the results the MEG had recorded. For the moment, all I could tell for sure was that our subjects really seemed to get a kick out of participating in this study. Or as one person exiting the machine put it, "Can I go again?" Each subject also expressed interest in hearing about the results when we were finished.

On the final day, we wrapped up our research by heading to a Mets game with the entire lab team. During the seventh inning, the famous "kiss cam" at Citi Field scanned the stands before stopping at Donald Trump and his wife, Melania Knauss-Trump—who happily obliged. The crowd went wild. We weren't the only ones in New York City that night interested in kissing.

So now it's time to turn to the outcome of the experiment—after one critical caveat, anyway. Before going into any further detail, it's necessary to be completely clear about what this work did, and perhaps, more important, did *not*, find. In fact, as kissing research proceeds in the future, such qualifications may become increasingly important, due to the sensitive, sexually charged nature of the topic and the strong possibility of popular and media misinterpretations.

Research on kissing will, from time to time, bring up the matter of differences of sexual orientation, both among study subjects and among kissing couples who are depicted visually (as in our neuroscience experiment). But that does not mean that our work in any way found, proved, or even suggested anything concrete or definitive about the differences between gay and straight people, whether in their behaviors, attitudes, motivations, or preferences.

The results obtained in both investigations did reveal some interesting, albeit very preliminary, trends. However, scientists are justifiably concerned about publicly reporting these trends, no matter how many caveats they include along with them.

The problem is that all too often, the news media latch on to a scientific finding to make it sound "sexy" in order to boost ratings or spin the story to suit a particular agenda. Even when researchers are very careful in what they say to the press, the results will frequently be overstated or misstated to make them sound bigger and more definitive, and less nuanced and less uncertain, than they really are. In some cases, very early scientific findings can be spun to the point of ridiculousness or even sheer falsity. When this occurs, it's no longer science reporting, but entertainment and (quite honestly) dollars to the media industry.

Moreover, such "journalism" can be particularly damaging when it comes to matters of human sexuality, where many people already have strong biases and preconceived notions. So with all of that said, let me be unequivocal: Our neuroscience experiment does not show that there is something fundamentally different between gay kissing and straight kissing. Instead, it merely opens the door to the next set of questions to explore.

That said, here's what happened...

· · ·

DAVID AND GREGORY tirelessly analyzed the data using a computer program called MEG160, which works by filtering and averaging together all of the results. A few weeks after the scans took place, they called me to discuss the findings. It turns out that they were far more intriguing than any of us had anticipated.

Two unexpected trends emerged among our volunteer subjects. First, the photographs of same-sex couples kissing resulted in a stronger magnetic field recorded in the MEG than the photographs of opposite-sex couples. What this means is that when a particular same-sex image was displayed, the study subjects generated a greater brain response than they did when looking at opposite-sex couples. This held true regardless of whether the couples in the images were male-male or female-female, and regardless of whether they were engaged in an "erotic," "friendship," or "relationship" kiss. Moreover, in statistical terms, the results were highly significant, meaning that some factor must account for the differences we observed.

But why was everyone showing a stronger response to homosexual kisses, even those among apparent friends? The most plausible explanation could be cultural: Our volunteers probably encounter male-female kissing more often in public and in the media than same-sex kissing. Therefore, the differences we observed in the experiment could be due to the frequency with which we see similar events in our actual lives.

In neuroscience, there's even a name for this phenomenon: a "frequency effect." It means that the more something is encountered, the smaller the response it evokes in our brain. MEG experiments on language recognition, for instance, have demonstrated that rarely used words elicit a much stronger response than common words. For example, because we hear the word "table" so often, a subject hearing it in an MEG machine generates a much smaller magnetic field than when hearing a far less commonly used word, like "ibex."

The second result was even more puzzling. The timing of the brain's first response to each image also varied strongly depending on whether it depicted an opposite- or same-sex kiss. Male-male and female-female kissing alike elicited a much faster brain reaction in the test subjects. While David and Gregory found this fact intriguing, they say it's very hard to interpret, and is not necessarily evidence of any inherent bias or prejudice. Once again, the quicker reactions may reflect the fact that same-sex kissing was a less ordinary occurrence for our subjects to behold. The difference in responses may also have been due to other factors in the photos, such as lighting and edges, because the MEG response is extremely sensitive. So in sum, we observed an interesting pattern, but more research is required to start developing theories on why it occurred.

Before we ran the MEG, my hypothesis had been that different kissing types might influence the strength of a subject's reaction, and that erotic kisses would evoke the strongest ones. I also suspected that male volunteers would show a greater response than women, because they are more sensitive to visual stimuli. I included images of same-sex couples to add more variety to the photographs, not because I wanted to test the difference between reactions to same-sex and opposite-sex kisses.

And yet when the results came back, there was no difference in responses among male and female test subjects, or based on whether the kisses in the pictures were erotic or not. Rather, the results showed a notable difference in brain response to opposite- and same-sex kissing. It was a classic case of scientific research surprising you and leading you in a very new direction—raising many new questions in the process. In other words the experience was a dramatic example of how science is *supposed* to work.

In popular television dramas, science is always portrayed as if mysteries are solvable in an hour or so—or at least within a few episodes. But real science just doesn't work that way. Our MEG experiment broke new ground by investigating kissing in a way that's never been done before, at least so far as we can tell. It was a first step in the hope of finding out whether further investigation is worthwhile— which it *definitely* is. The science of kissing is in its formative years, and there is vastly more to do, both inside MEG machines and elsewhere.

For precisely this reason, though, scientists cannot go

around drawing rash conclusions about human sexuality or behavior based on one preliminary experiment involving a very limited number of participants. Instead, we must use the results as clues to help design the next stage of investigation.

What's next? Well, since we now know that small factors in the photographs can affect brain responses, a future study might create a new set of images that more carefully control for differences in background, lighting, contrast, and other attributes, including the people shown. This way, the photographs would be more standardized to make all the conditions as similar as possible, except for the specific factor we're most interested in examining (i.e., what the response is to an erotic versus a friendship kiss, or to a same-sex versus opposite-sex kiss). Then, if researchers continue to see the same trends in subsequent controlled trials, we might develop much firmer ideas about what's occurring.

We might also choose our study participants more carefully in a later test. For example, if the difference between the reaction to opposite- and same-sex kissing was indeed a product of the frequency effect, it's possible that people who, say, spend hours each week staring at homosexual images (like homosexual pornography) would not show as strong a response to same-sex kisses. That would be a notable finding.

In short, when we ran the kissing experiment, we saw an interesting pattern that strongly suggests more research would be a good idea. One day, we may be able to identify a compelling neurological basis for the different reactions recorded in the MEG scanner—but in the meantime we have already developed some important ideas about how to approach the next set of intriguing questions in brain-kissing research.

And so, the science of kissing continues. Indeed, it is really just getting started.

Kissing and the Brain

*T*hroughout our lives, the physical structure of the brain's neural network is continuously changing as we experience the world, and the new neural connections formed can be strengthened over time with experience.

When we kiss another person—especially someone new—there's a lot of information being processed: his or her scent, taste, movement, touch, and even sound. This information helps the brain interpret the way we think and feel about this individual by associating these sensations with him or her. So as we kiss, we alter our brain. Changes occur on a microscopic scale (as they do with any other activity), but it's fair to say that in this manner, kissing can literally reshape the mind.

CHAPTER 11

The Open Lab

The neuroscience experiment described in the previous chapter ventured into just one field of many in which scientific research on kissing can evolve. The possibilities of where it may go from here are vast and virtually limitless. At the conclusion of any scientific paper, it is customary to highlight a field's outstanding questions and potential new directions. So now that we have explored kissing's history and evolution, its incarnations across species, and its effects on our bodies, let's try to predict what comes next. Here I will describe some potential experiments worth pursuit that tie together themes across disciplines, building on the most intriguing aspects of what has gone before.

1. OUR KISSING COUSINS

Chapter 2 journeyed around the animal kingdom for a colorful sampling of kissing-like behaviors in our close and distant relatives. The species whose kisses seemed the most similar to our own was an amorous primate cousin, the bonobo, whose pink lips and dexterous tongue can be used to express all manner of affectionate social behaviors. Since the study of the relationship between hormones and kissing in humans has proven difficult—apparently due to the stresses of an unnaturally clinical testing environment—it's possible that research on bonobos may shed new light on our outstanding questions.

To find out, anthropologists and endocrinologists might collaborate, starting from the foundation laid down by Wendy Hill and Carey Wilson of Lafayette College. As discussed in chapter 8, their team used saliva and blood samples to measure oxytocin and cortisol levels in couples before and after kissing sessions, with the expectation that kissing would decrease stress and increase the flow of hormones associated with emotional attachment. To remove the influence of experimental anxiety, a similar study could be undertaken in bonobos under natural conditions. As a result, scientists might develop a more complete understanding of the role of kissing in their social interactions—and by extension, greater insight into our own.

How could the study work? Scientists already working with sanctuary bonobos would have to gather hormone samples from subjects well accustomed to frequent kissing sessions in that setting. Certainly they would not feel as uncomfortable or as anxious as the Lafayette College students, and therefore data should be more reliable.

The methodology for obtaining it is not difficult: In the past few years, hormone tests have been conducted on bonobos' saliva by giving them cotton swabs coated in powdered SweeTarts. Once the sugar is gone and the cotton discarded, swabs are collected and analyzed. So theoretically this procedure could be combined with simple blood tests to measure oxytocin and cortisol levels before and after a pair is observed to tongue-kiss. If scientists were to record a rise in oxytocin and a drop in cortisol, it might demonstrate the importance of kissing for developing and maintaining social bonds in a closely related species. This would provide greater evidence that humans and bonobos kiss for similar reasons and possibly suggest that kissing's true nature may be even more universal than we currently acknowledge.

2. NO ASSEMBLY REQUIRED

The simple action of tilting our head prior to kissing can actually offer some valuable clues about nonverbal communication between people. University of Chicago psychologist Howard Nusbaum suggests that conducting a study that recruits volunteers to kiss in the lab might allow social scientists to observe how this phenomenon works. If strangers bump heads more frequently than couples in established relationships, scientists might conclude that experience matters. However, research on other gestures has demonstrated the way that humans are extremely good at picking up on instantaneous nonverbal cues. So familiarity with a kissing companion may not be particularly important.

In addition, some participants could be required to remember a series of numbers (this is known as a "cognitive load") to determine if a mental task results in a higher collision rate, since concentration shifts. Finally, one person in an established couple might be instructed to initiate a kiss in the opposite than normal direction to find out whether a partner can easily accommodate the switch.

Although head tilt may seem perfunctory, it may be useful to help scientists explore the significance of the way we interpret simple social cues from others and how that informs our actions.

3. THE CONTEXT OF KISSING

While it would be extremely difficult, if not impossible, for two people to kiss in a brain scanner, we may yet be able to use brain imaging technology to learn more about the neuroscience of kissing; namely, how the context in which a kiss occurs influences the overall experience.

In chapter 5, we saw that during a kiss, many cues are transmitted that help our brains and bodies figure out what to do and influence the neurotransmitters regulating how we feel and behave. All the many and varied elements that make up the environment in which a kiss occurs—mood,

ambiance, strength of the connection between two people—
thus play a critical role in the outcome of any exchange. At
the most basic level, the recipient has to interpret the origins
of the kiss—including whether it is delivered from a friend,
lover, or enemy. This information then influences the way
he or she reacts. And while the methodology to study this
process may not be simple, it is probably possible by using
an fMRI machine.

Previous research on pain response has demonstrated
that the presence of a loved one can reduce the severity of
discomfort. In a 2006 study, for instance, sixteen married
women were put in an fMRI machine knowing they would
feel an electric shock on their ankle while holding the hand
of either their husband, an anonymous male experimenter,
or neither. This was the first experiment documenting the
way that touch can affect brain response to a threatening
situation. Happily married women reporting the highest
levels of relationship satisfaction and holding the hands of
their husbands experienced the least discomfort during the
experiment. In other words, knowledge about who is present
in the environment interacts with a person's physiology to
determine how he or she ultimately experiences a situation.
This relates to why, when it comes to kissing, the identity of
the other person has a strong influence on how we feel.

Once again, there's a technological constraint here—we
cannot fit two heads in an fMRI scanner. However, hand-
kissing might serve as a workable alternative to investigate

how our response to a kiss varies based on the person who delivers it. As we observed in chapter 3, hand-kissing has been recorded since antiquity. So using a methodology modeled after the fMRI hand-holding experiment described above, a similar study could investigate how the kissing experience is influenced by the kisser's identity. Like the women in the previous experiment, subjects in the fMRI machine would be told who is kissing their hand (a spouse or a stranger). By monitoring brain activity, scientists would then be able to observe how the response varies depending upon the relationship between the subject in the machine and kisser. If different responses are noted after repeated trials among many test subjects, this kind of investigation may finally be able to show that a kiss is not "just a kiss," but rather highly dependent on the context in which it occurs.

4. THE TEST OF TIME

Another intriguing area would be to examine attitudes on kissing over time in relationships. After all, the bond between two people can transform tremendously as partners undergo significant life changes. Some couples grow together over time, others apart. By learning about the role of kissing as relationships and their participants mature, we might be able to provide couples with better guidance, especially for keeping a marriage together and understanding the physical and emotional needs of another person at different stages of life.

To find answers to these types of questions, scientists could conduct what's called a longitudinal study—one that follows the same individuals over a long time. They could ask men and women questions about their kissing preferences very similar to the ones asked in the Albany social survey described in chapter 6: what appeals to them in a kiss, what they notice most about a kissing partner, how significant they consider kissing to be in their committed relationships, sexual encounters, and so on. By continuing to survey the same subjects at five-year intervals, we might start to observe trends in how perspectives on kissing change over time. The interviews might begin when the subjects are college-aged, but the continual stream of data would ultimately cast light on the preferences of both genders as we age.

Longitudinal research in other closely related areas suggests that in such a study, scientists might find distinct differences. For example, would the value one places on kissing frequency and intensity decrease for men and women as family responsibilities generally pile up toward middle age? By eighty, might participants find amusement looking back at what motivated them to kiss another person in their twenties?

On a related note—and while this might be scientifically challenging—it would be highly illuminating to obtain hormonal data on the very same subjects, so as to observe how the bodies of each participant changes alongside his or her responses. After all, relationships ebb and flow along with physical intimacy. Perhaps we would see that changes in kissing preferences are associated with increased or decreased testosterone and estrogen levels, or observe women's attitudes notably shifting post-menopause. This kind of investigation could provide insight into the influence of the aging process on how we foster important social bonds with loved ones and teach scientists more about what may be involved in the success of a long-term commitment.

Of course, while such data are certainly not unobtainable, we would inevitably have to wait a very long time—and depend on a very committed team of researchers—in order to learn from them. But it would be interesting to test whether kissing between two people in a decades-long happy marriage promotes higher oxytocin levels than kissing between members of a young couple early on in their relationship. These studies could be tweaked to consider multiple theories about kissing, stress, and attachment.

The results really matter when you consider the longevity of relationships. Most of us hope to make a lifelong commitment at the altar, but divorce statistics around the world demonstrate that unfortunately, many are unable to follow through. If research is able to demonstrate that physical intimacy—measured by factors such as the frequency of kissing—is correlated with increased relationship satisfaction, then it's possible some type of "kissing therapy" might even be incorporated into marriage counseling.

5. FOLLOW YOUR NOSE

Olfaction provides yet another area where kissing related research has miles to go. As highlighted in chapter 7, scientists already have much evidence suggesting that our sense of smell plays a large role in our decision to venture into a romantic relationship. It may even provide a means of assessing another partner's genes, and particularly his or her major histocompatibility complex, or MHC.

But the MHC is only one part of our very vast human genome. The real relationship between our sense of smell, our genes, and compatibility is likely far more complex and involves many other regions. As geneticists learn more about the roles of different human genes in the coming years, they may also find a firmer physiological basis for understanding how our scent preferences play a role in choosing a partner, and why or if such choices matter down the line, when children come along.

6. DIVERSITY MATTERS

When the methods of hormonal experimentation are refined, it would be interesting to study subjects from various age groups and a diversity of backgrounds, clarifying whether their results might apply to a larger demographic than the limited sample studied at one university.

In chapter 6, we learned that heterosexual men and women express different preferences about kissing style. This likely relates both to hormones and to cultural expectations, so it would be very illuminating to look more closely at how a person's sexual orientation may play a role in his or her attitudes toward kissing. Consider perhaps a large social survey, similar in style to the one given at the University at Albany, but including members of every community— lesbian, gay, heterosexual, bisexual, and transgender.

Likewise, we have seen how kissing customs and styles vary tremendously around the world. The same survey may therefore yield distinct results in different countries. For example, would men in Brazil, India, and China report the same preference for tongue-kissing that American men seem to enjoy? Would teeth be as significant to women in Australia, Japan, and Spain? Despite physiological similarities, I strongly suspect that culture would influence the results, but this has not yet been tested scientifically.

WHO CAN SAY WHERE kissing research will go from here? If you were to map out the course of scientific progress for any discipline, the resulting diagram would look like a branching tree. Some limbs would break or die off as studies hit roadblocks or as the scientific community lost interest. Meanwhile, other limbs would continue to grow in all sorts of unpredictable directions, as science bursts forth to accommodate emerging ideas.

With this image in mind, my hope is that I have highlighted some of the outstanding questions, and so may inspire new research avenues for others to pursue, particularly in neuroscience. After all, while kissing hasn't been fully ignored by modern scientific investigators, it also hasn't received very much attention. Perhaps we're beginning to see that change.

CHAPTER 12

The Future of Kissing

The kiss's popularity and appeal has changed through-out history, often as a result of shifting social mores and cultural norms. Just as nineteenth-century explorers brought the behavior to people around the world, television and film expanded its exposure in the twentieth century. Today, the human population is moving and networking faster than ever before, and kissing customs and opportunities continue to be in a state of flux thanks to emerging technologies. So we'll now examine how kissing may be changing in the twenty-first century as we glimpse into the future.

The research I've highlighted emphasizes the significance of kissing in relationships, so it's worth considering how the dating landscape is changing in our increasingly wired society. Many people are looking to the Web in search of partners through sites like Match.com, eHarmony .com, and others. And no wonder: It's fast, efficient, and the singles pool seems virtually limitless.

Online daters get to know each other's "personalities" via their profiles long before they venture into close proximity. On the surface, it may seem like a great way to weed out bad matches while retaining a very large selection of potential partners to choose from. Yet there are also some notable drawbacks that should be obvious at this point in the book. Although the Internet is a wonderful innovation, it does not provide the opportunity to sample the scent, taste, and other nonverbal cues emanating from those across the screen. These naturally important signals are entirely absent from a digital "wink," "poke," "flirt," or whatever means is used to initiate the first communication. As a result, it forces us to make decisions without the instincts that have evolved to guide us best. Dates are selected without visual, tactile, and other clues guiding users. So in a sense, when we're dating online, we're flying blind—or at least handicapped—due to such limited information compared to an in-person encounter.

On top of that, the factors that traditionally spark our interest in someone are likely less obvious on the Internet, as greater emphasis is placed on superficial attributes or a carefully worded profile. Research on online dating trends has revealed that a person's apparent physical attractiveness (based on a photograph or written description) is most influential in terms of the number of interested emails he or she receives. For example, men who report being six foot three or six foot four on their profiles receive more contact than average, while women seem to get the most attention when they are between five foot three and five foot eight. Meanwhile, red-haired men and gray- or short-haired women fare worse than average, and blondes or women with long, straight hair have an advantage.

This creates the incentive to lie about appearances, and many users do so hoping to increase the number of potential matches interested in meeting them. Men will often add extra inches to their height, while women are likely to whittle off several pounds in their stated description. Thus not only are behavioral and other signals unavailable, but the information being used to judge a person's potential suitability is often skewed.

Still, do these observations constitute a significant hurdle to the future of relationships? Probably not. A positive interaction online will eventually lead to a real date offline where more reliable information can be conveyed, and daters quickly discover the truth. Additionally, the singles pool on the Web is larger than would occur in a physical setting, so even unintentionally weeding out some well-suited matches might not prove that much of a drawback. Finally, online dating has other benefits balancing out the equation. For instance, if potential couples get to know each other adequately before going in for their first kiss, the chances of a positive connection may be improved since they are more comfortable together. Once partners have begun to develop a bond, the associated hormonal changes in their bodies boost the likelihood that a physical relationship will feel right.

But it is still worth questioning how this relatively new trend may be affecting human courtship behavior, like kissing, that has evolved over millions of years to help identify a suitable mate. We may invest a significant amount of time learning about a person who's not a good match. So in the end, the moment our lips touch probably reveals more about actual chemistry than weeks of accumulated emails. Still, at the very least, connecting online can increase our opportunities to get that close in the first place.

And when it comes to new frontiers in romantic technology, dating websites are just the beginning. The gaming world is booming as platforms improve and virtual experiences become ever more interactive. For example, Second Life, the Internet's largest user-created 3-D community, abounds with kisses between avatars in serious and casual relationships. Just as in the real world, kissing is a favorite activity in virtual life.

In 2009, Nintendo DS debuted a Japanese computer game called *Love Plus*. It's not the first dating video game, but its release raised eyebrows around the world as players were required to kiss their digital girlfriends. These kisses merely required tapping the screen with a stylus rather than a player's actual lips, but the enormous popularity of *Love Plus* suggests that as engineering improves and computer graphics become ever more believable, there is an audience

ready to embrace virtual relationships—quite literally—
including the act of kissing an animated character.

So what about off the screen? Computer scientists are
giving us a sneak peek at what may be next on the horizon
in the evolution of kissing—robots that kiss one another or,
perhaps someday, kiss us.

In 2008, the world saw the debut of Taiwan's kissing
robots, "Thomas" and "Janet." These somewhat lifelike
machines were designed to "kiss" at the National Taiwan
University of Science and Technology. They are, reportedly, the first robotic pair to lock lips, an action involving
complex hand-eye coordination and precise balance.

Thomas and Janet are part of a group of perform-
ing robot actors, but might this new technology suggest
more about what's to come? Although these bots are not
intended for human interactions, it's possible that comput-
ers could eventually look and act convincingly enough to
serve as surrogate human partners. Androids (male robots)
and gynoids or fembots (female robots) have been depicted
in films such as *Millennium Man*, *A.I.*, and *Austin Powers*.
As science advances, there is anticipation of more realistic
intimate physical interactions with them. But the notion of
kissing machines that have been programmed to simulate us
is no longer just part of science fiction.

In 2010, a full-sized female companion robot, named
"Roxxxy," debuted at the Adult Video News Adult Entertainment Expo. Touted as the world's first robotic girl-

friend, she stands five feet seven inches tall and weighs 120 pounds. Roxxxy's computer employs speech-synthesis and voice-recognition software, and according to the website she

> knows your name, your likes and dislikes, can carry on a discussion and expresses her love to you and be your loving friend. She can talk to you, listen to you and feel your touch. She can even have an orgasm!

It certainly sounds intriguing, but can she *kiss*?

To find out, I called the company. It turns out Roxxxy has a motor in her mouth with sensors, but cannot take an active role in kissing. Instead, her mouth was designed to be pleasurable for other oral purposes. Like the rest of her, it was molded from the body of a female fine arts model, and serves as one of three "inputs" for users.

Roxxxy's engineers predict that companion robots will become commonplace in people's homes over time. Since presumably her main buyers are men—who, as we've seen, do not generally place very high significance on kissing—most will probably not miss the activity. However, TrueCompanion.com is currently preparing to release a male sex robot named "Rocky." Will a stronger female market request an enhanced kissing feature? There are currently no plans to develop this kind of function, but they carefully consider feedback when deciding on future updates. However, even if scientists engineer the perfect kissing robot, it would lack a human element that is impossible to program: the ability to form real lasting social bonds.

EVERY DAY, new technologies change the way we interact with the world, from how doctors cure disease to the ease with which we stay connected to our social network. So although it's not possible to predict exactly what's in store for kissing in the future, we can already imagine some interesting possibilities. Perhaps it will be possible to "kiss" a loved one through the computer, or maybe virtual technology will allow us to experience the kiss of a celebrity or idealized partner. Just as with inventions like space shuttles and smart phones, the coming decades will reveal new kissing technologies that we can't begin to imagine in the present day. Still, there's one thing to be sure of: The kiss as we know it will never go out of style, because it promotes an important connection. But on a personal level, the meaning of a kiss will continue to change—just like our relationships.

A Look Back in Time

O nline dating has emerged recently, but advertisements for romance that feature kisses have been around for a long time. Nineteenth-century newspapers frequently included love notes, marriage proposals, and missed connections from singles in burgeoning cities. According to Rutgers historian Pam Epstein, they became so popular that there was even a manual available on how to compose a reply. This ad appeared in the New York Herald *on March* 20, 1870, *page* 1:

Will the lady with dark hair, to whom, while at a window with a friend this (Friday) morning, a card was shown, kindly send her card to the gentleman, whose name her friend knows? He regrets that he is compeled [sic] to resort to this method of making the request, but trusts that, under the circumstances, she will excuse and permit him (mentally) to kiss her hand.

No word on whether the lady with dark hair ever replied or received his kiss in person. ≈

CHAPTER 13

The Right Chemistry

From Cleopatra to Casanova, we remember those who were legendary for the art of seduction. But can science help us understand what they seem to have known intuitively—or at the very least guide us toward leaving the most lasting impression with our lips?

The truth is, it depends. A scientific understanding of endocrinology, olfaction, and other subjects can surely help improve the chances that a first kiss will go well, by making us more aware of how we may be affecting a partner. Science may give us an advantage, then; but how we use it is another matter, and the facts alone cannot provide the perfect ingredients to win someone's heart and be unforgettable. That takes charm and a fair amount of serendipity.

We kiss to express affection, adoration, respect, and love. We kiss to celebrate new beginnings and to say goodbye. We kiss because we care, or want to appear to. It all results in a staggering amount of brain activity and many complex changes in our bodies. I'll end this final chapter with some very concrete tips about how, based on the latest science, to be a better kisser—but first let's survey how far we've journeyed.

When it comes to kissing, we've seen that millions of years of evolution are working to direct us. Peering across the animal kingdom demonstrates the remarkable power of physical displays of affection—often of a kissing-like nature—to connect individuals in strong relationships. Though we vary from our mammalian relatives in many respects, in the end humans work in very much the same way. We need to share, to connect, to communicate beyond just using language; and kissing has been a dramatically successful means of doing so.

Today we see kissing practically everywhere, albeit in highly varied forms across the globe. It is a perfect example of how both "nature" *and* "nurture" combine to create a single complex and variable behavior, in this case one that fosters intimate social bonds among its practitioners—bonds we depend on for love, support, security, and even survival.

We've also seen that when we kiss, our bodies instinctively know a great deal about what to do and how to respond to another person. We collect a staggering amount of sensory data throughout the experience, and that data in turn set off a cascade of electrical and chemical reactions, which then modulate our behavior and help us decide whether the kiss *works* and whether we want to continue or go even further.

All of this unfolds at incredible speed in ways that

science has barely begun to understand. After all, and as we've seen, research on the brain's response to kissing barely exists in the scientific literature, and the results revealed by New York University's MEG machine raise many new questions. Research on kissing is just getting started, and we can assume that over the coming decades we'll know vastly more than we do at present.

Still, we're now in a position to at least take a crack at answering the questions we asked at the beginning of the book, based on the work of Niko Tinbergen, about why humans kiss.

"ULTIMATE" EXPLANATIONS

∽ WHERE DID KISSING COME FROM?

Other species, including many primates, engage in behaviors that are remarkably similar to what we call "kissing." Indeed, our close relatives, bonobos, quite literally kiss mouth-to-mouth, just as we do.

Animals engage in kissing-like behaviors for a wide range of reasons, from expressing affection to a simple greeting. Some animal "kisses" probably help promote special relationships between mothers and offspring, or between members of the same troop. In other cases, many species engage in a kissing-like motion to deliver chewed food to their young—and some human cultures also continue this practice today.

All of this affirms that what we call "kissing" has a deep biological history and is certainly not limited to humans. Rather, the broad distribution and persistence of this behavior suggests it plays a key role in holding individual members of different species together in romantic pairs, in family units, or in social groups.

In ancient humans or their ancestors, kissing may have first emerged from a search for sustenance and sex, from sniff greetings, from the feeding relationship between mother and child, or perhaps a combination of all three. We can't say for certain, but each possibility is supported by the observation of similar behaviors or displays in other species. One thing is for sure: Kissing worked, and it stuck. It is both ancient and common around the world, although different styles have gone in and out of fashion depending on events and sociocultural norms.

∾ How does kissing benefit us?

Like sex, romantic kissing is a behavior that facilitates reproduction. In this sense, its relationship to success in the competition to pass on one's genetic material is obvious. Kissing benefits us by helping us live on, through our genes, in our immediate offspring and beyond.

Seen in this light, many aspects of the kissing experience appear explicitly engineered to ensure reproductive success. For humans especially, female lips—much like female breasts and buttocks—serve to attract members of the opposite sex, acting almost as a kind of bull's-eye. The larger and redder they appear, the more attractive men seem to find them.

Actress Mae West once said, "A kiss is a man's signature." She was right. Besides mere attraction, there's a subtler way in which the kissing experience guides our reproductive decisions even further. A good deal of the scientific literature speculates that kissing may have evolved to help us choose a suitable partner, or to realize when a match is a bad idea. Kissing may serve as an investigative tool that brings us close enough to taste, smell, and interpret cues from a partner, so as to assess the potential for a relationship. The exchange of olfactory, tactile, and postural information might trigger unconscious mechanisms that guide us in deciding whether we should continue, and a kiss might even tell us about a potential partner's level of commitment and genetic compatibility.

These unconscious cues probably work for both sexes, but in different ways. For men, a larger and plumper female mouth is attractive—and that's probably no accident. Large lips may subconsciously inform a man of a woman's fertility or her health.

A woman, in turn, can tell a great deal about her partner by his kiss, even if she's not aware of it. Her body may react to the taste of his lips, his tongue, and his testosterone-laden saliva, as well as the way he positions his body—all of which help her decide whether he's worth mating with.

Meanwhile, her acute sense of smell might offer additional information, particularly if his natural odor provides a window onto his genes and whether potential children from this union will have a strong immune system.

Both partners, then, have hidden skills to help them evaluate the other through a kiss. So in a sense, their kiss can serve as nature's litmus test of their relationship and whether it will produce healthy offspring. That's quite a benefit—to us, and to our species.

"PROXIMATE" EXPLANATIONS

℘ WHAT MOTIVATES US TO KISS?

Romantic kissing usually occurs when two individuals share a sense of closeness and intimacy. The precise trigger for this behavior varies from relationship to relationship, but always involves complex biological, physical, and social influences. Perhaps most important is a combination of craving and emotional attachment spurred on by the neurotransmitters and hormones in our bodies, such as dopamine and oxytocin. These substances promote a sense of desire and anticipation. They also encourage us to keep going when the match and moment are right.

Context is also extremely important for eliciting a kiss. For the first kiss especially, a comfortable and secure environment encourages the exchange. And no wonder: Research suggests that kissing reduces the body's levels of cortisol, a stress hormone. A good kiss brings the sense of relaxation, as well as positive feelings of reward and security, thus reinforcing the behavior and leading to further kisses.

✑ HOW DO WE KNOW HOW TO KISS?

Kissing may be learned early, through the affection expressed by family and friends toward a young child. Even in infancy, the manner in which a mother presses her lips to an infant to kiss or feed stimulates pleasure centers in the baby's brain. So does nursing. These sensations may lay down an early cognitive map for the positive feelings associated with kissing that will later emerge in adult relationships.

However, such early experiences are by no means required to join the international kissing community. Nor do they always imply that a child will express love through the lips as an adult. In several cultures that do not traditionally kiss on the lips in a romantic fashion, individuals have nevertheless been observed to premasticate meals, or to kiss children as a sign of adoration.

Today, kissing is so ingrained in most societies that it is nearly impossible to avoid encountering it. There can be little doubt that in the United States our urge to kiss is strongly influenced by Hollywood, fairy tales, people we see on the street, and the chatter among peers as we're growing up. We see kissing on television, on billboards, and at school. We read about it in novels and magazines. The behavior is better advertised than Coca-Cola.

All of these influences lead us to want to kiss, to feel it's something we should do to express love, and to "know" that it should be done in a mouth-to-mouth fashion (even though not all human cultures have agreed). Thus it is from the complex interplay between our biology, our psychology, and our cultural expectations that the knowledge of how to kiss has emerged.

THAT'S WHERE SCIENCE STANDS on kissing—but it's not the only kind of information this book intends to convey. Let's face it: We want to be memorable kissers, and I would be extremely remiss not to close with some scientifically based tips. To that end, here are ten lessons that emerge directly from the science discussed in the preceding pages. Some may sound familiar, but they take on new resonance and force once you recognize the science behind them.

1. PLAY UP YOUR ASSETS—WISELY. Certain cosmetics serve to make our lips more alluring for a very good reason: Men like lips, and they like them red. So if makeup is your style, a little gloss or shine may send the right signals, making you look your most alluring.

But at the same time, the research also suggests not to overdo it. Lipstick appeals to a very primal urge, but men don't like a fake-looking pout. Moderation is critical. Evolution has made our lips naturally seductive no matter what we do—so long as we don't go too far in making a spectacle out of them.

2. IMPROVE YOUR TASTE AND SCENT. Taste and smell can make a big difference in the kissing experience and serve to lure in the opposite sex. So if you want to be a memorable kisser—in a positive way—you should brush and floss your teeth every day to keep the bacteria in your mouth in check. In particular, it is critical to ward off the gum disease gingivitis, which can leave you with chronic bad breath, missing teeth, and even an increased risk of heart disease.

Although some odors are beyond our control, you can further stack the odds in your favor by avoiding certain spicy or strong foods. Keep a breath mint or chewing gum nearby, in case you have not had time to properly prepare for a fortuitous kissing encounter.

3. GET TO KNOW EACH OTHER. If you want your first kiss with a partner to be magnificent, it's crucial to spend lots of time learning about each other first, so as to lay down the right hormonal foundation. In the process, both of you will be building a bond with a strong chemical basis. In particular, you need to encourage the firing of those hormones that foster feelings of attachment and adoration, so that you each develop an emotional

investment that sets the stage for a physical connection. That way, by the time things move to the next level, oxytocin will already be your ally—and kissing may only reinforce the closeness you already share.

4. FOSTER ANTICIPATION. Yearning for something makes finally getting it all the better, and a kiss is no exception. If Rhett had kissed Scarlett in the opening scene of *Gone With the Wind*, audiences wouldn't have remained nearly so invested in what happened to the couple after that. It was far better to watch the sexual tension build—and in our own lives, feelings work precisely the same way.

The first kiss will be most pleasurable if each person has been dreaming about how, when, and where it will take place. When both individuals feel the thrill of the chase, the result upon final contact could be of the kind that poets describe with violins and fireworks.

That's the romance novel version of this advice, but the science backs it up: Even when you've already got oxytocin on your side, you still need dopamine to foster desire. Before a kiss, you want this neurotransmitter spiking to its highest levels yet—at least before things get more physical.

That's why a fumbling drunk cannot seriously expect his sloppy kiss to impress a stranger (unless perhaps she's equally drunk). By contrast, a couple that talks and flirts for hours in a comfortable setting builds up anticipation. By getting to know each other, they begin to pick up subtle clues about whether the other person is interested. The boundaries of personal space break down as a bond begins. When they finally kiss, the dopamine reward for each will be greater, and the kiss will be all the more memorable.

5. MAKE KISSING COMFORTABLE. Setting the scene is very important to ensure that a kiss goes well, because we strongly associate a good kiss with feelings of security and trust. For the same reason, worrying too much about all the details is counterproductive—cortisol and kissing just don't match. Stress might ruin the moment before it arrives, or prevent it from happening in the first place.

Not every aspect of a kiss is under your control, but you can definitely boost the likelihood that it will go well. So wait until the mood feels right, and at all costs, don't rush. When both people feel relaxed and comfortable together, the time is ideal for making a move.

6. THE POWER OF TOUCH. As we've observed, our lips have evolved to be one of our body's most sensitive areas, bringing us pleasure with the lightest brush. Even slight pressure will launch an electric light parade of impulses in the brain and once we have sampled the sensations that can ensue, we crave more. Kissing is like a drug,

sending us on a natural high that can be better than any recreational substance. The associated hormones promote our desire to continue.

Still, if you want your partner's lips to enjoy your kiss, don't forget to pay attention to other parts of his or her body as well—preferably before the kiss itself happens. Caressing a partner's back or face can send a cascade of pleasurable signals to the brain, while subduing each person's level of cortisol and putting you both at greater ease. Hugging, hand-holding, and massage can similarly foster positive feelings of attachment and even love. Tactfully surprising a partner in this manner may make the kiss feel even better, as dopamine revs into high gear because of the added novelty.

7. TRUST YOUR BODY. If a kiss feels "right," continue. If you sense something's off, it may be your body's natural way of saying "stop!" Perhaps you and the person you're kissing have similar immunities, and you somehow sense that this individual would not make a good mate genetically.

For just as practicing good hygiene is critical to kissing success, the research suggests that even so, it might not be enough. It's always possible that your particular scent or taste just won't sit right with your partner, for reasons that our conscious minds can neither understand nor control. Or vice versa. When a kiss does not go as well as you may have hoped, remember there is someone else out there just waiting for you and your chemistry to come along.

8. DON'T RUIN THE MOMENT. There are numerous ways to spoil even the most promising kiss. Avoiding most of them is simply common sense, but understanding the science involved helps as well.

For example, never push another person's boundaries too far, making him or her feel insecure and more guarded—you're triggering the wrong hormones. Instead, be as reciprocal as possible, paying attention to a partner's response without dominating the exchange. Most important, do not overanalyze the situation, but instead let your body take over. Thinking too much will not let you fully experience the moment. Permit yourself—brain and body—the freedom to enjoy the kiss.

Also, remember that alcohol and drugs can alter the kissing experience. So for that critical first one to be memorable, make sure it's the kiss, rather than chemical substances, that makes it feel good. Otherwise the intense feelings of a special connection may dissipate as their effects wear off.

9. DON'T JUST BE A "GOOD KISSER," BE A GOOD KISSER FOR YOUR PARTICULAR PARTNER. When two people become accustomed to kissing, they grow attuned to

each other's body language and desires. This means that those we remember most may not have had their technique down to a universal art, but rather were probably gifted at understanding *us* and when the environment was right to move in. The "best" kissers keep a mate satisfied because they are emotionally and physically receptive to the other person, making him or her feel adored.

To maximize a passionate kissing response, then, it's best to work at open communication in all aspects of a relationship. A good match depends on far more than compatible kissing. Common values, shared experiences, sensitive timing, and compatible goals can make the difference between a fleeting experience or lifetime commitment. Above all, trust and honesty between two people allow them to develop a deep sense of what the other person needs.

10. KISS REGULARLY AND OFTEN. Once you've found someone special, a kiss works to maintain the strong partnership you share by helping to keep passion alive—with plenty of assistance from those hormones and neurotransmitters. Lots of kissing is a telltale sign of a healthy relationship, because the connection fosters a sense of security through companionship—which in turn has been physiologically linked to happiness.

At the close of this journey, we have begun to understand a great deal of the science of kissing. But as with most endeavors of this sort, we're also left with more questions and avenues worth pursuing.

What science has only begun to explore, with some fancy tools and lots of fresh ideas, poets and artists have already sought to comprehend for millennia, writing sonnets and creating masterpieces based on this single theme. Explorers, too, pondered the strange kissing-like behaviors they observed around the globe. As "enlightened" Europeans, they felt their particular form of kissing made them superior. Today, by contrast, we know that kissing is a practice echoed across the animal kingdom and that in fact it unites people rather than dividing them.

If there's a single message you take away from this book, I hope it will be this: Don't give up on romance. A kiss can be one of the most extraordinary shared experiences between two people and understanding the science behind it can help to improve each moment.

On the Science of Kissing

When it comes to matters of the heart, the kiss has evolved to foster feelings of connection, romance, and intimacy—feelings that, when the match is right, may be promoted indefinitely between individuals. It can be scientifically investigated, studied, and even dissected from every angle, but in the end we're left with one real and firm conclusion. Kissing is a type of universal language, best interpreted by those involved in the exchange.

And so the kiss persists through time, over generations and among peoples, across latitudes and longitudes. It will continue to motivate lovers, actors, writers, and all of us. For no matter how it began, why we do it, and where it takes place, a kiss often celebrates perhaps the greatest emotion of all: love.

Acknowledgments

I could not have completed this book without the support of so many individuals who guided me along the journey. For helpful readings, feedback, and advice, I'd like to thank my longtime colleague and dear friend Chris Mooney. His thought-provoking ideas frequently found their way into the manuscript as my research progressed, and it is with Chris's encouragement that I've evolved from scientist to writer.

I am also extremely grateful to Vanessa Woods for support and companionship during long hours writing together. Our afternoon conversations often led to serious questions investigated in the book. Vanessa's work and research on bonobos particularly helped to inform chapters 1 and 2. Thanks also to her husband, Duke anthropologist Brian Hare. He illuminated many ideas included on animal behavior and provided excellent insight into the lives of dogs and primates.

Vilayanur S. Ramachandran deserves credit for

suggesting that I consider the science of kissing seriously as a book idea, and I am grateful for his support.

Thanks to Al Teich and Jill Pace for co-organizing the 2009 American Association for the Advancement of Science symposium on "The Science of Kissing." Many thoughtful discussions with them about the role of science in society influenced the topics covered.

I am indebted to anthropologist Vaughn Bryant and classicist Donald Lateiner for providing me with a very vast amount of information about the history of kissing. They brought chapters 3 and 4 to life with fascinating anecdotes from the literature. Tremendous thanks as well to my wonderful agent Sydelle Kramer, who helped foster early ideas and develop questions to pursue. Also to my fantastic editor Emily Griffin, for adding greater depth and dimension to each chapter, and Roland Ottewell, for scrupulous attention to details.

I'm grateful to Stuart Pimm and members of the Duke community for workspace and stimulating conversations about science, kissing, and the science of kissing. Thanks to Austin Luton for help with translations, fact-checking, and assisting with the editing process. Also to Michael Nitabach, Helen Fisher, Gordon Gallup, Sarah Woodley, Lawrence Krauss, Melissa Bates, Bethany Brookshire, Tara Smith, Howard Nusbaum, John Bohannon, Catharine and Bora Zivkovic, and Yuying Zhang for answering my technical questions related to their expertise. Thanks to Pam

Epstein for providing historical context for the *New York Herald* newspaper advertisement. And to Michael Burkley, John Renish, Jessica Franken, Geran Smith, and Joseph Flasher, for volunteering to help with research online.

For photographs and art, I'm grateful to Nicolas Devos, Wim Delvoye, Vanessa Woods, Ariel Soto, Marika Cifor, Alexandra Williams, the Space Telescope Science Institute, and the London Museum of Natural History. Also to *Discover* magazine's Web editors Amos Zeeberg and Gemma Shusterman, who have organized a "Science of Kissing Gallery" to feature collected kisses from across time, space, and species (http://blogs.discovermagazine.com/intersection/science-of-kissing-gallery/). Additionally, Amos and our *Discover* magazine colleague Eliza Strickland were kind enough to participate in the MEG kissing experiment featured in chapter 10.

Tremendous thanks to David Poeppel and his incredible lab at New York University, who collaborated with me in developing the neuroscience study. This group deserves very special recognition for taking my idea seriously enough to bravely run the kissing experiment. The team offered endless hours of time, patience, and encouragement, and I learned a great deal from our work together. Gregory Cogan helped enormously with data analysis and provided fine hospitality during my visit to New York University. He also assisted with the neuroscience information throughout the book. Thanks to Katherine Yoshida for guiding the methods of the investigation, Jeff Walker for running the MEG, Christine Boylan for measuring my head, Tobias Overath for safely sending me through the fMRI machine, additional lab members Xing Tian and Yue Zhang, and the hundreds of *Discover* magazine blog readers who participated in my preliminary kissing survey.

This book would not have been possible without a lifetime of love from Mom, Dad, Seth, Jen, and Rose. Thanks also to Rebecca McElroy for decades of informal discussion on the subject and Samantha Brooke, Benjamin Baron-Taltre, and Dan Cashman for encouragement when I needed it most.

Finally, very special thanks to my husband and muse David Lowry. He read many early versions of this manuscript, offering an interesting perspective that led to several new directions as I continued writing. An amazing field and lab biologist, he often helped get the details right whenever I had questions. David provides unending support for even my most outlandish ideas with boundless optimism, enthusiasm, and love.

Bibliography

Abbey, A., P. McAuslan, T. Zawacki, A. Clinton, and P. Buck. (2001) Attitudinal, experiential, and situational predictors of sexual assault perpetration. *Journal of Interpersonal Violence* 16: 784–807.

Adams. J. M. (1994) Will loggers put Koko out of the mood? *Baltimore Sun.*

Aiello, L., and C. Dean. (1990) *An Introduction to Human Evolutionary Anatomy.* New York: Academic Press.

Alter, R., J. Flannagan, and J, Bohannon. (1998) The effects of arousal on memory for first kisses. Paper presented at SEPA, Mobile, AL.

Altman, L. K. (1990, May 20) Henson death shows danger of pneumonia. *New York Times.*

Andrews, P. W., S. W. Gangestad, G. F. Miller, M. G. Haselton, R. Thornhill, and M. C. Neale (2008). Sex differences in detecting sexual infidelity: Results of a maximum likelihood method for analyzing the sensitivity of sex differences to underreporting. *Human Nature* 19: 347–373.

Angier, N. (1991, January 22) A potent peptide promotes an urge to cuddle. *New York Times.*

Archer, C. I., J. R. Ferris, H. H. Herwig, and T. H. E. Travers. (2008) *World History of Warfare*. Lincoln: University of Nebraska Press.

Arnold, K. A., and J. Barling. (2003) Occupational stress in "dirty work." In M. F. Dollard, H. R. Winefield, and A. H. Winefield, eds., *Occupational Stress in the Service Professions*. London: Taylor and Francis.

Aron, A., and E. N. Aron. (1991) Love and sexuality. In K. McKinney and S. Sprecher, eds., *Sexuality in Close Relationships*. Hillsdale, NJ: Erlbaum.

Aron, A., H. Fisher, D. Mashek, G. Strong, L. Haifang, and L. Brown. (2005) Reward, motivation, and emotion systems associated with early-stage intense romantic love. *J Neurophysiol* 94: 327–337.

Bailey, K. V. (1963) Premastication of infant food in the New Guinea Highlands. *South Pacific Comm Techn Inform Circ* 1:3.

Balcolmbe, J. (2006) *Pleasurable Kingdom: Animals and the Nature of Feeling Good*. London: Macmillan.

Barber, N. (1995) The evolutionary psychology of physical attractiveness: Sexual selection and human morphology. *Ethology and Sociobiology* 16: 395–424.

Barrett, D., J. G. Greenwood, and J. F. McCullagh. (2006) Kissing laterality and handedness. *Laterality* 11(6): 573–579.

BBC News. (2003, February 13). Kissing couples turn to the right. http://news.bbc.co.uk/2/hi/health/2752949.stm.

Benton, D. (1982) The influence of androstenol—a putative human pheromone—on mood throughout the menstrual cycle. *Biological Psychology* 15, no. 3–4: 249–256.

Berlin, B., and P. Kay. (1969) *Basic Color Terms: Their Universality and Evolution.* Berkeley: University of California Press.

Berscheid, E. (2003). The human's greatest strength: Other humans. In U.M. Staudinger, ed., *A Psychology of Human Strengths: Fundamental Questions and Future Directions for a Positive Psychology*, pp. 37–47. Washington, DC: American Psychological Association.

Biesbrock, A. R., M. S. Reddy, and M. J. Levine. (1991) Interaction of a salivary mucin-secretory immunoglobulin A complex with mucosal pathogens. *Infect Immun* 59(10): 3492–3497.

Bloch, I. (1934) *Odoratus Sexualis.* New York: Panurge Press.

Blue, A. (1997) *On Kissing: Travels in an Intimate Landscape.* New York: Kodansha International.

Brand, G., and Millot, J.-L. (2001) Sex-differences in human olfaction: Between evidence and enigma. *Quarterly Journal of Experimental Psychology B*, 54(3): 259–270.

Brewis, J., and S. Linstead. (2000) *Sex, Work and Sex Work: Eroticizing Organization.* New York: Routledge.

Brody, B. (1975) The sexual significance of the axillae. *Psychiatry* 38: 278–289.

Brown, R. (1974) Sexual arousal, the Coolidge effect and dominance in the rat (Rattus norvegicus). *Animal Behaviour* 22(3).

Bullivant, S. B., S. A. Sellergren, K. Stern, N. A. Spencer, S. Jacob, J. A. Mennella, and M. K. McClintock. (2004) Women's sexual experience during the menstrual cycle: Identification of the sexual phase by noninvasive measurement of luteinizing hormone. *J Sex Res* 41: 82–93.

Buss, D. (2003) *The Evolution of Desire: Strategies of Human Mating.* New York: Basic Books.

Buss, D. M. (2006). Strategies of human mating. *Psychological Topics* 15: 239–260.

Buss, D. M., R. Larsen, J. Semmelroth, and D. Westen. (1992) Sex differences in jealousy: Evolution, physiology, and psychology. *Psychological Science* 3: 251–255.

Buss, D. M., and T. K. Shackelford (1997). From vigilance to violence: Mate retention tactics in married couples. *Journal of Personality and Social Psychology* 72: 346–361.

Carpenter, J., J. Davis, N. Erwin-Stewart, T. Lee, J. Bransford, and N. Vye. (2009) Gender representation in humanoid robots for domestic use. *International Journal of Social Robotics* 1(3).

Changizi, M. A., Q. Zhang, and S. Shimojo. (2006) Bare skin, blood, and the evolution of primate colour vision. *Biology Letters* 2: 217–221.

Chayavichitsilp, P., J. V. Buckwalter, A. C. Krakowski, and F. Friedlander. (2009) Herpes simplex. *Pediatr Rev* 30: 119–130.

Coan, J. A., H. S. Schaefer, and R. J. Davidson. (2006) Lending a hand: Social regulation of the neural response to threat. *Psychological Science* 17 (12): 1032–1039.

Cogan, G., K. Yoshida, S. Kirshenbaum, and D. Poeppel. Towards a taxonomy of kissing: MEG responses to complex visual scenes of osculatory behavior. In prep.

Corsini, R. (1999) *The Dictionary of Psychology*. New York: Routledge.

Coryell, J. F., and G. F. Michel. (1978) How supine postural preferences of infants can contribute toward the development of handedness. *Infant Behaviour and Development* 1: 245–257.

Crawley. E. (1925) *Studies of Savages and Sex*. Edited by T. Besterman. Whitefish, MT: Kessinger Publishing 2006.

Cunningham, M. R., A. R. Roberts, A. P. Barbee, P. B. Druen, and C. Wu. (1995) Their ideas of beauty are, on the whole, the same as ours: Consistency and variability in the cross-cultural perception of female physical attraction. *Journal of Personality and Social Psychology* 68: 261–279.

Darwin, C. (1872) *The Expression of the Emotions in Man and Animals*. Chicago: University of Chicago Press.

De Waal, F. B. (1982) *Chimpanzee Politics: Power and Sex Among Apes*. New York: Harper and Row.

————. (1990) *Peacemaking Among Primates*. Cambridge, MA: Harvard University Press.

————. (1997) *Bonobo: The Forgotten Ape*. Berkeley: University of California Press.

————. (2000) Primates: A natural heritage of conflict resolution. *Science* 289: 586–590.

Dirks, T. M (n.d.) Best and Most Memorable Film Kisses of All Time in Cinematic History. American Movie Classics Filmsite. http://www.filmsite.org/filmkisses.html.

Dixson, A. F. (1983) Observations on the evolution and behavioral significance of "sexual skin" in female primates. *Advances in the Study of Behavior* 13: 63–106.

Dixson, A. (1998) *Primate Sexuality: Comparative Studies of the Prosimians, Monkeys, Apes, and Human Beings*. New York: Oxford University Press.

Donaldson, Z. R., and L. J. Young. (2008) Oxytocin, vasopressin, and the neurogenetics of sociology. *Science* 322: 900–904.

Doty, R. L. (1976) *Mammalian Olfaction, Reproductive Processes, and Behavior*. New York: Academic Press.

Doty, R. L., P. Shaman, S. L. Applebaum, R. Giberson, L. Siksorski, and L. Rosenberg. (1984) Smell identification ability: Changes with age. *Science* 226: 1441–1443.

Doty, R. L., M. Ford, G. Preti, and G. R. Huggins. (1975) Changes in the intensity and pleasantness of human vaginal odors during the menstrual cycle. *Science* 190: 1316–1317.

Dubuc, C., L. J. N. Brent, A. K. Accamando, M. S. Gerald, A. MacLarnon, S. Semple, M. Heistermann, and A. Engelhardt. (2009) Sexual skin color contains information about the timing of the fertile phase in free-ranging Macaca mulatta. *J Primatology* 30: 777–789.

Durham, T. M. T. Mallot, and E. D. Hodges. (1993) Halitosis: Knowing when "bad breath" signals systemic disease. *Geriatrics* 48: 55–59.

Dwyer, K. (2005) *Kiss and Tell: A Trivial Study of Smooching*. Philadelphia Quirk Books.

Eibl-Eibesfeldt, I. (1970) *Love and Hate: On the Natural History of Behavior Patterns*. London: Methuen.

————. (1977) Patterns of Greeting in New Guinea. In S. A. Wurm, ed., *New Guinea Area Languages and Language Study*, vol. 3, pp. 209–247. Canberra: Australian National University.

Eimer, M. (2000) Effects of face inversion on the structural encoding and recognition of faces: Evidence from event-related brain potentials. *Cognitive Brain Research* 10(1–2): 145–158.

Ekman, P. (1993) Facial expression and Emotion. *American Psychologist* 48: 384–392.

Elder, J. (2005) An 'Eskimo kiss' is a kunik, and maybe not what you think. *South Coast Today*. http://archive.southcoasttoday.com/daily/02-05/02-16-05/b06li596.htm.

Ellis, H. (1936) *Studies in the Psychology of Sex*. New York: Random House.

Enfeild, J. (2004) *Kiss and Tell: An Intimate History of Kissing.* New York: HarperCollins.

Engert, F. B., and T. Bonhoeffer. (1999) Dendritic spine changes associated with hippocampal long-term synaptic plasticity. *Nature* 399: 66–70.

Etcoff, N. (1999) *Survival of the Prettiest: The Science of Beauty.* New York: Doubleday.

Ferrari, P. F., V. Gallese, G. Rizzolatti, and L. Fogassi. (2003) Mirror neurons responding to the observation of ingestive and communicative mouth actions in the monkey ventral premotor cortex. *European Journal of Neuroscience* 17: 1703–1714.

Fisher, H. E., (1992) *Anatomy of Love: A Natural History of Monogamy, Adultery, and Divorce.* New York: Norton.

————. (1994) *Anatomy of Love: A Natural History of Mating, Marriage, and Why We Stray.* New York: Ballantine.

————. (1998) Lust, attraction, and attachment in mammalian reproduction. *Human Nature* 9: 23–52.

Fisher, H. E., A. Aron, D. Mashek, G. Strong, H. Li, and L. L. Brown. (2002) Defining the brain systems of lust, romantic attraction and attachment. *Archives of Sexual Behavior* 31: 413–419.

Foer, J. (2006, February 14) The kiss of life. *New York Times.*

Ford, C. S., and F. A. Beach. (1951) *Patterns of Sexual Behavior.* New York: Harper and Row.

Fouts, R., and S. T. Mills. (1998) *Next of Kin.* New York: Harper Paperbacks.

Freud, S. (1962) *Three Essays on the Theory of Sexuality.* Trans. James Strachey. New York: Basic Books.

Fullagar, R. (2003) Kiss me. *Nature Australia* 27: 74–75.

Ganapati, P. (2009, August 26) Humanoid robots share their first kiss. Wired Gadget Lab. http://www.wired.com /gadgetlab/2009/08/humanoid-robots-kiss/.

Gangestad, S. W., R. Thornhill, and C. Garver. (2002) Changes in women's sexual interests and their partners' mate retention tactics across the menstrual cycle: Evidence for shifting conflicts of interest. *Proc R Soc London B* 269: 975–982.

———. (2005). Adaptations to ovulation. In D. M. Buss, ed., *The Handbook of Evolutionary Psychology*, pp. 344–371. Hoboken, NJ: Wiley.

Garcia-Velasc, J., and M. Mondragon. (1991) The incidence of the vomeronasal organ in 1000 human subjects and its possible clinical significance. *Journal of Steroid Biochemistry and Molecular Biology* 39(4).

Garver-Apgar, C. E., S. W. Gangestad, R. Thornhill, R. D. Miller, and J. J. Olp. (2006) Major histocompatibility complex alleles, sexual responsivity, and unfaithfulness in romantic couples. *Psychological Science* 17(10): 830–835.

Geer, J., J. Heiman, and H. Leitenberg. (1984) *Human Sexuality*. Englewood Cliffs, NJ: Prentice Hall.

Giannini, A. J., G. Colapietro, A. E. Slaby, S. M. Melemis, and R. K. Bowman. (1998) Sexualization of the female foot as a response to sexually transmitted epidemics: A preliminary study. *Psychological Reports* 83(2): 491–498.

Gilad, Y., V. Wiebe, M. Przeworski, D. Lancet, and S. Pääbo. (2004) Loss of olfactory receptor genes coincides with the acquisition of full trichromatic vision in primates. *PLoS Biol* 2.

Goodall, J. (2000) *Through a Window: My Thirty Years with the Chimpanzees of Gombe*. New York: Mariner.

Goodchilds, J. D., and G. L. Zellman. (1984) Sexual signaling and sexual aggression in adolescent relationships. In N. Malamuth and E. Donnerstein, eds., *Pornography and Sexual Aggression*, pp. 233–243. Orlando, FL: Academic Press.

Gower, D. B., and B. A. Ruparelia. (1993) Olfaction in humans with special reference to odours 16-androstenes: Their occurrence, perception and possible social, and sexual impact. *J Endocrinol* 137: 167–187.

Grammer, K. (1993) 5-a-androst-16en-3-a-on: a male pheromone? A brief report. *Ethology and Sociobiology* 14: 201–208.

Gray, J. (1993) *Men Are from Mars, Women Are from Venus: A Practical Guide for Improving Communication and Getting What You Want in Your Relationships*. New York: HarperCollins.

Griggs, B. (2010, February 1) Inventor unveils $7,000 talking sex robot. CNN.

Gulledge, A.K., M. H. Gulledge, and R. F. Stahmann. (2003) Romantic physical affection types and relationship satisfaction. *American Journal of Family Therapy* 31: 233–242.

Güntürkün, O. (2003) Human behaviour: Adult persistence of head-turning asymmetry. *Nature* 421(6924).

Hallett, R., L. A. Haapanen, and S. S. Teuber. (2002) Food allergies and kissing. *New England Journal of Medicine* 346: 1833–1834.

Hamann, S., R. Herman, C. Nolan, and K. Wallen. (2004) Men and women differ in amygdala response to visual sexual stimuli. *Nature Neuroscience* 7: 411–416.

Hamer, D. (2002) Genetics of sexual behavior. In J. Benjamin, R. Ebstein, and R. Belmaker, eds., *Molecular Genetics and the Human Personality*, pp. 257–273. Washington DC: American Psychiatric Publishing.

Harmetz, A. (1985, October 31) A rule on kissing scenes and AIDS. *New York Times*.

Harvey, K. (2005) *The Kiss in History*. Manchester, UK: Manchester University Press.

Haselton, M. G., and S. W. Gangestad (2006) Conditional expression of women's desires and men's mate guarding across the ovulatory cycle. *Horm Behav* 49: 509–518.

Haselton, M. G., M. Mortezaie, E. G. Pillsworth, A. E. Bleske-Recheck, and D. A. Frederick. (2007). Ovulation and human female ornamentation: Near ovulation, women dress to impress. *Hormones and Behavior* 51: 40–45.

Hatfield, E., and S. Sprecher. (1986) Measuring passionate love in intimate relationships. *J Adolesc* 9: 383–410.

Hawley, R. (2007) "Give me a thousand kisses": The kiss, identity, and power in Greek and Roman antiquity. *Leeds International Classical Studies* 6.

Hitsch, G. J., A. Hortaçsu, and D. Ariely. (2006) What makes you click? Mate preferences and matching outcomes in online dating. MIT Sloan Research Paper.

Hold, B., and M. Schleidt. (1977) The importance of human odour in non-verbal communication. *Z. Tierpsychol* 43: 225–238.

Hopkins, E. W. (1907) The sniff-kiss in ancient India. *Journal of the American Oriental Society* 28: 120–134.

Hoshi, K., Y. Yamano, A. Mitsunaga, S. Shimizu, J. Kagawa, and H. Ogiuchi. (2002) Gastrointestinal diseases and halitosis: Association of gastric Helicobacter pylori infection. *International Dental Journal* 52: 207–211.

House, J. S., K. R. Landis, and D. Umberson. (1988) Social relationships and health. *Science* 241: 540–545.

Howard, C. J. (1995) *Dolphin Chronicles*. New York: Bantam.

Hughes, S. M., M. A. Harrison, and G. G. Gallup Jr. (2007) Sex differences in romantic kissing among college students: An evolutionary perspective. *Evolutionary Psychology* 5(3): 612–631.

Jankowiak, W. R., and E. F. Fischer. (1992) A cross-cultural perspective on romantic love. *Ethnology* 31: 149–155.

Johnston, V. S., and M. Franklin. (1993) Is beauty in the eye of the beholder? *Ethology and Sociobiology* 14(3): 183–199.

Jones, D. (1996) *Physical Attractiveness and the Theory of Sexual Selection*. Ann Arbor: Museum of Anthropology, University of Michigan.

Jones, S., R. Martin, and D. Pilbeam. (1992) *The Cambridge Encyclopedia of Human Evolution*. New York: Cambridge University Press.

Kell, C. A., K. von Kriegstein, A. Rösler, A. Kleinschmidt, and H. Laufs. (2005) The sensory cortical representation of the human penis: Revisiting somatotopy in the male homunculus. *J Neurosci* 25(25): 5984–5987.

Kiell, N. (1976) *Varieties of Sexual Experience*. New York: International Universities Press.

Kinsey, A. C., W. B. Pomeroy, and C. E. Martin. (1948) *Sexual Behavior in the Human Male*. Philadelphia: W. B. Saunders.

Kinsey, A. C., W. B. Pomeroy, C. E. Martin, and P. H. Gebhard. (1953) *Sexual Behavior in the Human Female*. Philadelphia: W. B. Saunders.

Kirk-Smith, M. D., and D. A. Booth. (1980) Effect of androstenone on choice of location in others' presence. In H. van der Starre, ed., *Olfaction and Taste VII*. London: IRL Press.

Kirshenbaum, S. (2009) K*I*S*S*I*N*G. *New Scientist*, Issue 2695.

Klein, S. (2006) *The Science of Happiness: How Our Brains Make Us Happy—And What We Can Do to Get Happier*. Translated by Stephen Lehmann. New York: Marlowe and Company.

Kluger, J. (2008, January 17) The science of romance: Why we love. Time.

Koelega, H. S. (1970) Extraversion, sex, arousal and olfactory sensitivity. *Acta Psychol* 34: 51–66.

Koelega, H. S., and E. P. Köster. (1974) Some experiments on sex differences in odor perception. *Ann NY Acad Sci* 237: 234–246.

Koss, M. (1988) Hidden rape: Sexual aggression and victimization in a national sample in higher education. In A. W. Burgess, ed., *Rape and Sexual Assault*, pp. 3–25. New York: Garland.

Lander, A. (2008, January 9) Will SA law steal teens' kisses? BBC News.

Laska, M., A. Seibt, and A. Weber. (2000) "Microsmatic" primates revisited: Olfactory sensitivity in the squirrel monkey. *Chem Senses* 25: 47–53.

Lateiner, D. (1995) *Sardonic Smile: Nonverbal Behavior in Homeric Epic*. Ann Arbor: University of Michigan Press.

———. (2009) Greek and Roman kissing: Occasions, protocols, methods, and mistakes. *Amphora* 8(1).

Laycock, T. (1840) *A Treatise on the Nervous Diseases of Women*. London: Longman.

Lazaridis, N. (2003) Sigmund Freud's oral cancer. *British Journal of Oral and Maxillofacial Surgery* 41(2): 78–83.

Lieberman, P. (1993) *Uniquely Human*. Cambridge, MA: Harvard University Press.

Liggett, J. (1974) *The Human Face*. New York: Stein and Day.

Light K. C., K. M. Grewen, and J. A. Amico. (2005) More

frequent partner hugs and higher oxytocin levels are linked to lower blood pressure and heart rate in premenopausal women. *Biological Psychology* 69: 5–21.

Lorenz, K. (1966) *On aggression*. London: Methuen.

Lounasmaa, O. V., M. Hämäläinen, R. Hari, and R. Salmelin. (1996) Information processing in the human brain: Magnetoencephalographic approach. *Proc Natl Acad Sci USA* 93(17): 8809–8815.

Lowenstein, L. F. (2002) Fetishes and their associated behavior. *Sexuality and Disability* 20(2).

McCabe, M. P., and J. K. Collins. (1984) Measurement of depth of desired and experienced sexual involvement at different stages of dating. *Journal of Sex Research* 20: 337–390.

McCann, A., and L. Bonci. N (2001) Maintaining women's oral health. *Dental Clinical North America* 45: 571–601.

McClintock, M. K. (1971) Menstrual synchrony and suppression. *Nature* 229: 244–245.

———. (1984) Estrous synchrony: Modulation of ovarian cycle length by female pheromones. *Physiology and Behavior* 32: 701–705.

Major, J. R. (1987) "Bastard feudalism" and the kiss: Changing social mores in late medieval and early modern France. *Journal of Interdisciplinary History* 17(3): 509–535.

Malinowski, B. (1965) *Sex and Repression in Savage Society*. New York: World.

Marazziti, D., and D. Canale (2004) Hormonal changes when falling in love. *Psychoneuroendocrinology* 29: 931–936.

Marazziti, D., H. S. Akiskal, A. Rossi, and G. B. Cassano. (1999) Alteration of the platelet serotonin transporter in romantic love. *Psychol Med* 29: 741–745.

Marshall, D. (1971). Sexual behavior on Mangaia. In D. Marshall and R. Suggs, eds., *Human Sexual Behavior*. New York: Basic Books.

Meisenheimer, J. (1921) *Geschlecht und Geschlechter im Tierreich*. Vol. 1. *Die naturlichen Beziehungen*. Jena: Fisher.

Meredith, M. (2001) Human vermonasal organ function: A critical review of best and worst cases. *Chem Senses* 26: 433–445.

Meston, C. M. (2000) Sympathetic nervous system activity and female sexual arousal. *American Journal of Cardiology* 86: 30F–34F.

Meston, C. M., and B. B. Gorzalka. (1996) Differential effects of sympathetic activation on sexual arousal in sexually dysfunctional and functional women. *Journal of Abnormal Psychology* 105: 582–591.

Meyer III, W. J., J. W. Finkelstein, C. A. Stuart, A. Webb, E. R. Smith, A. F. Payer, and P. A. Walker. (1981) Physical and hormonal evaluation of transsexual patients during hormonal therapy. *Archives of Sexual Behavior* 10(4).

Michael, R. P., R. W. Bonsall, and M. Kutner. (1995) Volatile fatty acids, "copulines," in human vaginal secretions. *Psychoneuroendocrinology* 1: 153–163.

Miller, G., J. M. Tybur, and B. D. Jordan. (2007) Ovulatory cycle effects on tip earnings by lap dancers: Economic evidence for human estrus? *Evolution and Human Behavior* 28(6): 375–381.

Mitchell, M. (1936) *Gone with the Wind*. New York: Macmillan.

Mollon, J. D. (1989) "Tho she kneel'd in that place where they grew..."—the uses and origin of primate colour vision. *J Exp Biol* 146: 21–38.

Montagna. W., and P. F. Parakkal. (1974) *The Structure and Function of Skin*. New York: Academic Press.

Monti-Bloch, L., and B. I. Grosser. (1991) Effect of putative pheromones on the electrical activity of the human vomero-nasal organ and olfactory epithelium. *J Steroid Biochem Mol Biol* 39(48): 573–582.

Morris, D. (1967) *The Naked Ape: A Zoologist's Study of the Human Animal*. New York: Bantam.

————. (1997) *Intimate Behavior*. New York: Kodansha Globe.

————. (2005) *The Naked Woman: A Study of the Female Body*. New York: Thomas Dunne Books.

Morrow, L. (2005, June 21) Changing the signals of passion. *Time*.

Morse, D. (2006) The stressful kiss: A biopsychosocial evaluation of the origins, evolution, and societal significance of vampirism. *Stress and Health* 9(3): 181–199.

Münte, T. F., B.M. Wieringa, H. Weyerts, A. Szentkuti, M. Matzke, and S. Johannes. (2001) Differences in brain potentials to open and closed class words: Class and frequency effects. *Neuropsychologia* 39(1): 91–102.

Nakamura, A., T. Yamada, A. Goto, T. Kato, K. Ito, Y. Abe, T. Kachi, and R. Kakigi. (1998) Somatosensory homunculus as drawn by MEG. *Neuroimage* 7(4): 377–386.

Nguyen, B. T., T. D. Tran, M. Hoshiyama, K. Inui, and R. Kakigi. (2004) Face representation in the human primary somatosensory cortex. *Neurosci Res* 50(2): 227–32.

Nicholson. B. (1984) Does kissing aid human bonding by semiochemical addiction? *British Journal of Dermatology* 111(5): 623–627.

Nunn, C. (1999) The evolution of exaggerated sexual swellings in primates and the graded signal hypothesis. *Animal Behaviour* 58: 229–246.

Nyrop, C. *The Kiss and Its History* (1901) Translated by W. F. Harvey. Whitefish, MT: Kessinger Publishing. 2009.

Ocklenburg, S., and Güntürkün, O. (2009) Head-turning asymmetries during kissing and their association with lateral preference. *Laterality: Asymmetries of Body, Brain and Cognition* 14(1): 79–85.

Osorio, D., and M. Vorobyev. (1996) Colour vision as an adaptation to frugivory in primates. *Proc R Soc Lond B Biol Sci* 263: 593–599.

Page, J. (2007, August 22) Father, 90, shows off new baby—and wants more. Times Online. http://www.timesonline.co.uk/tol/news/world/asia/article2302545.ece.

Paget, L. (n.d.) Kiss Your Way to Better Sex. Village. http://love.ivillage.com/lnssex/sexkissing/0,,nvv6-4,00.html.

Pallingston, J. (1998) *Lipstick: A Celebration of the World's Favorite Cosmetic*. London: St. Martin's Press.

Panati, C. (1998) *Sexy Origins and Intimate Things: The Rites and Rituals of Straights, Gays, Bis, Drags, Trans, Virgins, and Others*. New York: Penguin.

Pause, B. M. (2004) Are androgen steroids acting as pheromones in humans? *Physiology and Behavior* 83: 21–29.

Pause, B. M., B. Sojka, K. Krauel, G. Fehm-Wolfsdorf, and R. Ferstl. (1996) Olfactory information processing during the course of the menstrual cycle. *Biological Psychology* 44: 31–54.

Pedersen, C. A., J. A. Ascher, Y. L. Monroe, and A .J. Prange Jr. (1982) Oxytocin induces maternal behaviour in virginal female rats. *Science* 216: 648–650.

Perrett, D. I., K. A. May, and S. Yoshikawa. (1994) Facial shape and judgments of female attractiveness. *Nature* 368: 239–242.

Pfaus, J. G., T. E. Kippin, and G. Coria-Avila. (2003) What can animal models tell us about human sexual response? *Annu Rev Sex Res* 14: 1–63.

Pillsworth, E. G., M. G. Haselton, and D. M. Buss. (2004) Ovulatory shifts in female sexual desire. *Journal of Sex Research* 41: 55–65.

Polyak, S. L. (1957) *The Vertebrate Visual System*. University of Chicago Press.

Porter, R. H. (1999) Olfaction and human kin recognition. *Genetica* 104: 259–63.

Radbill, S. X. (1981) Infant feeding through the ages. *Clin Pediatr* 20(10): 613–621.

Ramachandran, V. S., and W. Hirstein. (1998) The perception of phantom limbs: The D. O. Hebb lecture. *Brain* 121: 1603–1630.

Reade, W. (1923) *The Martyrdom of Man*. Whitefish, MT. Kessinger Publishing.

Reed, J., J. Bohannon, G. Gooding, and A. Stehman. (2000) Kiss and tell: Affect and retellings of first kisses and first meetings. Paper presented at APS, Miami, FL.

Regan, B. C., C. Julliot, B. Simmen, F. Viénot, P. Charles-Dominique, and J. D. Mollon. (1998) Frugivory and colour vision in Alouatta seniculus, a trichromatic platyrrhine monkey. *Vision Res* 38: 3321–3327.

Rikowski, A., and K. Grammer. (1999) Human body odour, symmetry and attractiveness. *Proc R Soc Lond B* 266: 869–874.

Rizzolatti, G., L. Fogassi, and V. Gallese. (2000) Cortical mechanisms subserving object grasping and action recognition: a new view on the cortical motor function. In M. S. Gazzaniga, ed., *The New Cognitive Neurosciences*, 2nd ed., pp. 539–552. Cambridge, MA: MIT Press.

Rouquier, S., A. Blancher, and D. Giorgi. (2003) The olfactory receptor gene repertoire in primates and mouse: Evidence for reduction of the functional fraction in primates. *Proc Natl Acad Sci* 97: 2870–2874.

St. Johnston, A. (1883) *Camping Among Cannibals*. Macmillan.

Schaal, B, and R. H. Porter (1991) "Microsmatic humans" revisited: The generation and perception of chemical signals. *Adv Study Behav.* 20: 135–199.

Service, R. (1998) Breathalyzer device sniffs for disease. *Science* 281: 1431.

Setchell, J. M. (2005) Do females mandrills prefer brightly colored males? *Intl J Primatology* 26: 715–735.

Setchell, J. M., and A. F. Dixson. (2001) Changes in the secondary sexual adornments of male mandrills (Mandrillus sphinx) are associated with gain and loss of alpha status. *Hormones and Behavior* 39: 177–184

Shepherd, G. M. (2004) The human sense of smell: Are we better than we think? *PLoS Biol* 2(5).

Singh, D., and P. M. Bronstad. (2001) Female body odour is a potential cue to ovulation. *Proc R Soc Lond B* 268: 797–801.

Skipper, J., S. Goldin-Meadow, H. Nusbaum, and S. Small. (2009) Small gestures orchestrate brain networks for language understanding. *Current Biology* 19(8): 661–667.

Stein, M. L. (1974) *Lovers, Friends, Slaves...: The Nine Male*

Sexual Types, Their Psycho-Sexual Transactions with Call Girls. New York: Berkley.

Stephen, I. D., M. J. L. Smith, M. R. Stirrat, and D. I. Perrett. (2009) Facial coloration affects perceived health of human faces. *Int J of Primatology* 30: 845–857.

Stephens, T. C. (1917) The feeding of nestling birds. *Journal of Animal Behavior* 7. Number 4.

Stoddart, D. M. (1998) The human axillary organ: an evolutionary puzzle. *Human Evolution* 13(2).

————. (1990) *The Scented Ape: The Biology and Culture of Human Odour*. Cambridge, UK: Cambridge University Press.

Strovny, D. (n.d.) The orgasmic French kiss. *Men's Health*. http://www.askmen.com/dating/lovetip/35b_love_tip.html.

Swift, J., and T. Scott. (2009) *The Prose Works of Jonathan Swift*. vol. 11. *Literary Essays*. 1907. Whitefish, MT: Kessinger Publishing.

Symons, D. (1979) *The Evolution of Human Sexuality*. New York: Oxford University Press.

Tanikawa, M. (1995, May 28) Japan's young couples discover the kiss. *New York Times*.

Tennov, D. (1979) *Love and Limerence: The Experience of Being in Love in New York*. New York: Stein and Day.

Thornhill, R., and K. Grammer. (1999) The body and face of woman: One ornament that signals quality? *Evolution and Human Behavior* 20(2): 105–120

Thornhill, R., S. W. Gangestad, R. Miller, G. Scheyd, J. K. McCollough, and M. Franklin. (2003) Major histocompatibility complex genes, symmetry, and body scent attractiveness in men and women. *Behav Ecol* 14: 668–678.

Tierno, P. M., Jr. (2004) *The Secret Life of Germs: What They Are, Why We Need Them, and How We Can Protect Ourselves Against Them*. New York: Atria.

Tinbergen N. (1953) *The Herring Gull's World*. London: Collins.

————. (1963) On aims and methods of ethology. *Z Tierpsychol* 20: 410–433.

Tonzetich, J., G. Preti, and G. Huggins. (1978) Changes in concentration of volatile sulfur compounds of mouth air during the menstrual cycle. *Journal of International Medical Research* 6: 245–256.

Tournier, M. (1998) *The Mirror of Ideas*. Translated by J. Krell. Lincoln: University of Nebraska Press.

Trivers, R. (1972) Paternal investment and sexual selection. In B. Campbell, ed., *Sexual Selection and the Descent of Man*, pp. 136–179. New York: Aldine de Gruyter.

Tucker, R. K., M. G. Marvin, and B. Vivian. (1991) What constitutes a romantic act? An empirical study. *Psychological Reports* 69: 651–654.

Tully, J., R. M. Viner, P. G. Coen, J. M. Stuart, M. Zambon, C. Peckham, C. Booth, N. Klein, E. Kaczmarski, and R. Booy. (2006) Risk and protective factors for meningococcal disease in adolescents: Matched cohort study. *British Medical Journal* 332(7539): 445.

Turnbull, O. H., L. Stein, and M. D. Lucas. (1995) Lateral preferences in adult embracing: A test of the "hemispheric asymmetry" theory of infant cradling. *Journal of Genetic Psychology* 156 (1): 17–21.

Van Petten, C., and M. Kutas. (1990) Interactions between sentence context and word frequency in event-related brain potentials. *Memory and Cognition* 18(4): 380–393.

Van Toller, S., and G. H. Dodd. (1993) *Fragrance: The psychology and biology of perfume*. Springer.

Ververs, I. A. P., J. I. P. de Vries, H. P. van Geijn, and B. Hopkins. (1994) Prenatal head position from 12–38 weeks. I. Developmental aspects. *Early Human Development* 39: 83–91.

Vuilleumier, P., and G. Pourtois. (2007) Distributed and interactive brain mechanisms during emotion face perception: Evidence from functional neuroimaging. *Neuropsychologia* 45(1): 174–194.

Wagatsuma, E., and C.L. Kleinke. (1979) Ratings of facial beauty by Asian-American and Caucasian females. *Journal of Social Psychology* 109: 299–300.

Walter, C. (2008, February) Affairs of the lips: Why we kiss. *Scientific American*.

Wedekind, C., T. Seebeck, F. Bettens, and A. Paepke. (1995) MHC-dependent mate preferences in humans. *Proc R Soc Lond B* 260: 245–249.

William, C. (2009) Kissing. *New Scientist*, Issue 2720.

Woods, V. (2010) *Bonobo Handshake*. New York: Gotham.

Wrangham, R., and N. Conklin-Brittain. (2003) Cooking as a biological trait. *Comp Biochem Physiol A Mol Integr Physiol* 136: 35–46.

Yanoviak, S. P., M. Kaspari, R. Dudley, and G. Poinar Jr. (2008) Parasite-induced fruit mimicry in a tropical canopy ant. *American Naturalist* 171: 536–544.

Zahavi, A., and A. Zahavi. (1997) *The Handicap Principle: A Missing Piece of Darwin's Puzzle*. New York: Oxford University Press.

Index

Note: Italic page numbers refer to illustrations.

ABOUT THE AUTHOR

SHERIL KIRSHENBAUM is a research scientist at the University of Texas at Austin and a science journalist contributing to popular and academic publications from *The Nation* to *Science*. Her writing was featured in *The Best American Science Writing* 2010 anthology. A graduate of Tufts University, she holds two masters of science degrees in marine biology and marine policy from the University of Maine. Sheril has served as a science fellow on Capitol Hill and a pop radio jock, and currently co-hosts The Intersection on Discover blogs with Chris Mooney. She was born in Suffern, New York, and is also a musician.